HOW TO HAVE A GOOD LIFE IN A MESSY WORLD

ANCIENT WISDOM FOR MODERN LIVING

WILLARD BLACK

REALITY PRESS

HOW TO HAVE A GOOD LIFE IN A MESSY WORLD:
ANCIENT WISDOM FOR MODERN LIVING

WILLARD BLACK

Published in the United States by Reality Press
ISBN 978-0-9982103-1-5

Dedicated in memory of my late wife Mary Anne Black

Mother of Giselle, Eric, and Anya

Her children rise up and call her blessed:
her husband also, and he praises her:
"Many women do noble things,
but you surpass them all."

Proverbs 31

CONTENTS

ABOUT THIS BOOK
AND THE AUTHOR

Years ago, as a young college student, I enrolled in a class on Hebrew Wisdom Literature. I did so because I really liked the professor who taught it. He had a way of making the 3,000-year-old book of *Ecclesiastes* seem like a current best seller. He showed us how it revealed what is really important in life and what it takes to live a good life right now.

Later, in my 30's I met a wonderful woman in Colorado, Mary Fisher, who'd just turned 80. She was as vitally engaged in life and learning as any younger person I ever knew. One day, off the cuff, I asked her what she had to say about *life*. After a long, thoughtful pause, she declared, "Well, by the time you're 70 you finally know how to live. Then it's time to die."

The starkness of her answer prodded me to search deeper into Hebrew Wisdom Literature to see if I could change that short, sad timeline between finally becoming wise only when one faces the approach of death. Why not be wise all of one's life? Mary, by the way, lived to celebrate her 105th birthday, and I had the privilege to be there and reflect on other memorable conversations on this theme.

Eventually, I began giving seminars based on the timeless principles of *Ecclesiastes* that I titled *How to Live*. To my delight and surprise, I found that groups of people in such wildly diverse places as Staten

Island, New York; San Jose, California; Madison, Wisconsin; Vienna, Austria; and Warsaw, Poland, were all focused on similar themes in their own search for a good life.

That's what this book is about—a good life and the principles that, if followed, enable us to achieve such a life. This is not a scholarly exposition of *Ecclesiastes*, nor is it a text-by-text Bible study. It's about real-life topics that people want to talk about as they simply read *Ecclesiastes*. I suggest that you download and read the NIV (New International Version) translation of *Ecclesiastes* or another version of your choice if you do not have a Bible.

The author of *Ecclesiastes* was likely King Solomon of ancient Israel. The book's descriptions of the author's experiences fit Solomon's life and match the conditions of his period in Israel's history.

The subjects I've chosen for *How to Have a Good Life in a Messy World* have been gradually distilled since 1975 when I founded the Institute for Christian Resources, Inc., which is now known as Open Door Libraries (opendoorlibraries.org). This work is a non-profit organization designed to create seminars and workshops to deliver popular level applications of biblical principles on such down-to-earth issues as major life adjustments, family dynamics, effective parenting, successful marriages, current social issues, and dealing with loss, grief, and anger.

These issues became very personal for me. In 1976, I was suddenly widowed when my wife tragically died as the result of a viral streptococcus infection. Instantly I was thrust into the role of a single parent with children, ages 7, 12, and 14, at the very time I was creating a fledgling organization. As part of that work, I moved my children with me to Vienna, Austria, where I taught American college students living abroad. It was 1979, part of the Cold War era, and I also clandestinely taught national leaders behind the Iron Curtain.

My trips into Czechoslovakia, Romania, and Russia confirmed for me that the resource materials developed in distant California were a match for the people of the Soviet Bloc. A few years later when the Berlin Wall fell in 1989 and when the Soviet Union collapsed in 1990, many new and unforeseen opportunities emerged. With much help from many friends, I initiated the establishment of public Christian oriented libraries in Prague, Budapest, and Berlin, offering the best in Bible-based literature to populations long-starved for those resources.

In 2006 I returned to teaching as an adjunct instructor in the Inter-Cultural Studies Department of William Jessup University, just outside Sacramento, California.

How to Have a Good Life in a Messy World is my effort to share the insights I have gained from traveling, living, and teaching in various parts of the world—and from my own experiences of personal loss and personal fulfillment along the journey. Like you, dear reader, I've seen a lot and been through a lot. It's time for me, in some measure, to sum it all up.

As you read, I urge you to thoughtfully evaluate what it is that you are filling your life with right now. Decide where you are on the path to achieving a truly good life. Then think through what adjustments would make your life better. Finally, be energetic to follow through on the insights you gain.

There are countless "How To" books out there about finding happiness. Most of them rely on modern social theory and current behavioral research. I've read many of these books and find them useful. For this book, however, I have chosen to draw from the deep artesian well of ancient biblical wisdom and the pure, fresh water of inspired wise directives for carving out a good life from even the hardest circumstances. Best of all, I find that the long list of insights for good living found in *Ecclesiastes* is holistic, designed to meet our spiritual, social, psychological, and physical needs in full and in balance, without contradictions.

Fortunately for all succeeding generations, King Solomon, like his father, King David, was a prolific writer. But while David is known for his majestic Psalms, Solomon is known for his practical Proverbs. Solomon was famed for generously sharing the extraordinary wisdom he believed God had given him. This generosity was abundantly on display when the legendary Queen of Sheba made a state visit. The chronicle of that visit says, *"She came to Solomon and talked with him about all she had on her mind. Solomon answered all her questions; nothing was too hard for him to explain to her"* *(2 Chronicles 9:1, 2).*

Solomon, though wise, did have a problem. He was the dominant monarch in the Middle East during his 40-year reign. His military and political power was un-challenged. That meant he could do anything he wanted to—and he did. In spite of his wisdom, he willfully violated clear directives in the Law of Moses regard-ing the proper behavior of kings, both in the manage-ment of their governments and of their own personal behavior. That may be one reason why he wrote *Ecclesiastes,* both as a confession about the follies of his own life and about the true nature of life itself, which he called "life under the sun." As Solomon neared the end of his life, he reviewed and reflected on his many successes, mistakes, and indulgences. He concluded that much of what we restless humans think we want only ends in dissatisfaction and emptiness. The honesty with which he speaks to us would surely compel him to say, "Do as I said, not as I did." Faced with life's end, he became astoundingly clear about life's true purpose. From the ashes of faulty choices and futile pursuits, Solomon crafted one of the most significant documents ever written on understanding and fulfilling our true purpose here on earth.

Like Solomon, I am writing this book after decades of watching the validity of his observations played out, verified, and vindicated again and again in the last half of the 20th century and the first years of the 21st century, both in America and in other countries. My passion is to share the invaluable lessons I've learned from Solomon and from those who have shaped good lives by deliberately basing them on the principles of *Ecclesiastes*. I am both privileged and obligated to tell their stories and to share many of my own.

I find it especially helpful that *Ecclesiastes* does not discount life's messiness. To the contrary, it is addressed head on in terms so blunt they cannot be misunderstood. Therefore, I believe you will discover that your set of circumstances, no matter how seemingly unique or complex, will fit with the issues Solomon raised and the answers he offered in *Ecclesiastes*.

Indeed, Solomon shows us it is possible to get our arms around life at its worst and still make it meaningful. All of us have been or will be touched and perhaps tarnished by life's messes. Some of those messes may be terribly prolonged and horrifically difficult, especially the ones we bring on ourselves. Even then, though tempted by despair, Solomon says there are steps and actions to take to construct enough good to be able to say, "I have a good life."

But beware of comparisons. The good lives of others will likely look much different from yours. Secretly, however, all lives share much in common. It is those common factors I hope to help make your own, in part by presenting many real-life examples of success achieved in all circumstances. These examples, I believe, have the power to stir your courage and stimulate your creativity to forge ahead and find your own path to such success.

In facing life as it really is, I urge you to curb excessive optimism and to avoid undue pessimism. The first can divert you into unrealistic expectations. The second can cripple you with hopeless discouragement. It's a good piece of advice that says, "Most often the highs are illusory and the lows are illusory. Just keep on plugging."

Different kinds of wisdom are needed at different stages of life. If you are still in high school or even in the lower grades, if you are now in college or have just entered your first job, Solomon has a lot to say to you. I suggest you begin this brief book with the chapters that will help you immediately develop a clear sense of direction about the friendships you choose, the work you pursue, and the mate you select.

College, for example, exposes you to a blizzard of new information and diverse ideas about how to live and what to believe. When confronted so quickly by so much that is new and novel, it can be hard to keep your beliefs on a solid foundation and your behaviors on a steady course. Many modern professors go far beyond the academic goal of developing critical thinking and, instead, aggressively advance secularism and even Marxian Socialism as the so-called enlightened position of the truly educated. Behind the borders of countries where Marxism was practiced, I saw the results first hand – extreme shortages of medicines and available medical services, empty store shelves in grocery stores, and the longing for freedoms of association, speech and religion. Many professors do show a measure of respect for traditional views. College, in short, forces you to rethink your belief system and reexamine your world view, then either reaffirm or reject those positions for yourself. That's not all bad. The strongest plants often grow in the most hostile environments.

I also urge you younger readers to focus on the parts of this book that deal with the development of your character and your spiritual maturity. Who you are and what you become within yourself is far more important than what you achieve in the outside world. A wise job counselor said it well: "People get hired for their skills and fired for who they are." A teacher far wiser than Solomon has warned, *"What does it profit a man if he gains the whole world and loses his own soul."* No amount of outward success can compensate for inner failure.

After one's youth, the middle years of life, 35 to 55, are filled with swirls of activity, a host of relationships, and years of hard, demanding work. If you are there, I have shaped the content of this book to help you keep life in balance by altering the rhythms of your activities and responsibilities often enough to stay on top of things, which is a tall order at this stage of life. A key tactic in achieving such balance is to keep focus on the big picture and to press purposefully toward long-term goals.

In our later years, life is different but far from over. *Ecclesiastes* has much to teach us about discovering new goals, shaping fresh perspectives, and scaling back our activity to match our decline in energy. The wisdom that comes in our advancing years is, in fact, a wonderful compensation for the loss of youthful vitality. Such wisdom is urgently needed in today's youth-obsessed superficial society. America's indigenous peoples understood the vital importance of the "elders of the tribe" far better than we do. The young men were the tribe's hunters and warriors, meeting the tribe's immediate needs for food and for protection from marauding enemies. But the role of the elders was also important. It was their responsibility to take the long view—to see clearly and to plan wisely for what was needed for the tribe's long-range survival from generation to generation. Scripture, indeed, promises that the righteous influence of the wise elder will not diminish in old age but rather will steadily increase in the same way that the brightness of the sun reaches full strength as it makes it course across heavens.

Each chapter of this book stands independently. Each can be read separately. Each is a distinct presentation of what ordinary people living ordinary lives ask about, talk about, and wonder about when they read *Ecclesiastes*. Each is designed to stir serious reflection and even to ignite fierce resolve about how best to live well in this very messy world of the 21st century. I believe everyone wants a good life. I believe our Creator wants us to have a good life. I, too, want that good life for you. *Ecclesiastes* shows us how to achieve it.

ACKNOWLEDGEMENTS

"A friend is your needs answered." This insight of Lebanese poet and philosopher Kahlil Gibran came into play bigtime while writing this book. Vetting what went into print by people who knew the subject matter well and who understood where I was coming from were critical all of the way to the finish line. I appreciate their expertise and willingness to spend many hours evaluating manuscripts and advising on everything from arranging the order of the chapters to wordsmithing.

Phyllis Lanyon, Executive Director of Open Door Libraries, an international lecturer, a specialist in organizational management, and in an earlier career a high school English language teacher, was the ideal reader to detect grammatical errors and to improve clarity in expressing ideas. Phyllis is in life's trenches as a wife, mother, grandmother, and the director of a non-profit organization. That gives her a clear sense of what works and what doesn't in managing life.

Ron Wiebe, an advisor to Open Door Libraries, was the principal architect of the curriculum used by Open Door Libraries for training over 300 lay family counselors in Poland after the collapse of communism in Eastern Europe and Russia. Respected widely for both his family and corporate counseling skills, he assisted in refining human relations advice I offered for shaping good lives.

Merlynn Rosell Bergen, a cognition expert, helped identify what would help readers remember what is intended for them to learn from this book. Now retired, the bulk of her career was at Stanford University in the School of Medicine: Stanford Faculty Development Center. She directed an international program in Medical Decision Analysis for clinical teachers. Previously she taught statistics, measurement and research design for the Northern California extensions of both Fuller Seminary and Azusa Pacific University.

Al Kurz, a retired professor, Denver Seminary, who has taught extensively on *Ecclesiastes,* gleaned the manuscript for accuracy in interpretations of the passages chosen to develop the values that support good lives. This was critical in order to zero in on the best applications of wisdom articulated three thousand years ago.

Milton L. Pippenger, retired Superintendent of Schools in Hiawatha, Kansas and Garden City, Kansas received the honor of being named Kansas Superintendent of the Year 2000 and one of four finalists for National Superintendent in 2000. During periods of time between public school positions he was a professor at San Jose Christian College, San Jose, California, now William Jessup University, Rocklin, California, and Interim President of Manhattan Christian College, Manhattan, Kansas. While in San Jose he developed seminars sponsored by Open Door Libraries for parents on how to communicate with school teachers and administrators in order to receive the best learning results for their children. Interest in teaching *Ecclesiastes* in his church prompted him to create a workbook for teaching small groups and testing the concepts for a good life.

Don Clark, a retired journalist who has worked at the highest levels of excellence in all phases of his profession—newspapers, magazines, radio and television, most recently was the prize-winning senior television news anchor/reporter for the CBS affiliate television station, KBAK-TV, in Bakersfield, California. For *How to Have a Good Life in a Messy World* he offered suggestions for sharpening the descriptions of both my experiences and the experiences of others that were selected to illustrate ways to increase the probability of achieving a good life.

Carey Kinsolving, founder of Kids Talk About God, (KidsTalkAboutGod.org), was a freelance religion writer for the *Washington Post,* and also founded Faith Profiles.org/carey. As he read the manuscript, he pondered the question, "Will the reader turn the page?" He offered useful advice on the order of the chapters in the book.

Anita Callahan, now retired from the University of South Florida, was an Associate Professor of Industrial Engineering and Engineering Management. She was also on the faculty of the Honors College of the University of South Florida. During her tenure she also served as Associate Department Chair and Interim Department Chair of the Engineering Department. Before she and her husband moved from Silicon Valley to Florida, she gave seminars on Engineering Management Ethics, sponsored by Open Door Libraries. She has a keen sense of what works in imparting concepts for ethical behavior in the workplace and how to help women married to engineers from a wide variety of cultures manage differing beliefs about the role of women in the home and society. She could evaluate the book through that lens.

Paul B. Carroll, an award-winning reporter and editor for 17 years at the *Wall Street Journal* in the US, Europe and Latin America, is also the author of *Big Blues: The Unmaking of IBM* in 1993, *Billion-Dollar Lessons,* with co-author Chunka Mui, and The *New Killer Apps,* also co-authored with Chunka Mui. He gave three seminars which I attended on *How to Write a Book,* and I accepted his offer to contact him for advice in the process of writing this book. His seminar instruction at the beginning of this project and his personal guidance near the end kept me inspired and well directed to the very end.

Thank You, Friends. I needed you.
Willard Black

CHAPTER 1
TIMING IS OFTEN EVERYTHING

"There is a time for everything, a season for every activity under heaven" (Ecclesiastes 3:1).

WHEN you choose to do something is as important as WHAT you choose to do.

Matching action with timing leads to success in almost everything: relationships, sports, finances, even international affairs. In 1979, Egyptian President Anwar Sadat and Israeli Prime Minister Menachen Begin entered into a historic peace agreement. Later, when asked about this accomplishment, Sadat said if it had been three months earlier or three months later, this unprecedented breakthrough between the two nations would likely never have happened. It was only within a brief window of opportunity that Sadat, Begin, and U.S. President Jimmy Carter were aligned in their efforts. Only then were conditions mutually beneficial for both Egypt and Israel to take such bold action. Even now, in the 21st Century, world leaders still reflect on Anwar Sadat's legendary sense of timing. Forging this peace agreement was like a fast game of tennis, with both players striking the ball and making their moves with split-second timing. Three months earlier or three months later, it might never have happened.

Employers sometimes face the need to lay off employees. This is always an emotionally charged task in which poor timing can make things far worse than they need to be. Thoughtful employers make every effort to learn how best to perform this sad duty in a way that is honest, respectful, and sensitive to the need not to traumatize the employee in front of others or impair an employee's job prospects. If done right, both the boss's reputation and the employee's self-respect will be kept intact.

Remaining employees always face a new relational dynamic when someone from their group is forced to leave. When and how that change happens should be done in a way that is the least disruptive to them relationally and to their productivity. Look for the best times and keep in mind the worst times. A dismissal, for example, in the weeks just before Thanksgiving or Christmas would be seen as cruel and calloused, unless immediate action is absolutely required by a serious violation of company policies or moral standards. Otherwise, it can wait.

When asked about timing for firing, a retired manager of sales divisions in a major company said, "I chose early Friday afternoon because it impacted the rest of the sales force less than had I done it on Monday or Tuesday. The remaining employees did not have three or four days to discuss it at the water cooler, and the employee could experience less embarrassment. This avoided an otherwise built-in opportunity to stir up resentment against my leadership."

In situations within leadership teams where serious policy disagreements develop and continue, eventually someone has to go. If the people involved can communicate in a mature, civil manner, a mutual agreement on the departure time can be worked out amicably. Employees the next tier down can be tactfully informed about that agreement. I've seen that work well, but the key is for everyone to remain calm and not allow hurt or bitterness to stir up organizational turmoil. However, even at its best, this approach may not work for all groups.

In public schools, when cuts must be made in the teaching staff, pink slip warnings are sent approximately two months before the end of the school-year. Many teachers receive them, even though only a few may actually lose their jobs. The final decision on how many stay and how many go will be based on projected available funds and likely enrollment numbers. Even though it's disturbing to get a warning about possible job losses, this kind of advance advisory gives people time to look for other options and to plan for the best use of summer vacation time.

The timing, the wording, and the method of communicating the announcement of lay-offs or the delivery of pink slips should be done with sensitivity.

Timing can be significant even for less serious matters.

A friend in a foreign country tells a humorous story about his proposal to the woman he eventually married. It's Exhibit A on how to do a good thing with bad timing. While dating, he had watched several John Wayne movies. He resolved to make a dramatic proposal to his sweetheart based on what he saw on the American silver screen. Around midnight, he went to the street below her apartment. When he got her attention and she opened the window, he got down on his knees in the street and sonorously asked, "Will you marry me?" She bluntly answered, "Do you know what time it is?" and closed the window. Eventually he got his timing right. They are now married and have a couple of children.

A time to be silent and a time to speak up.

This element of timing is universally challenging. A quick thinking fellow recast this biblical text by saying, "Silence is golden, but sometimes it's plain yellow."

The Columbia Shuttle astronauts possibly could have been saved in 2003 if enough NASA engineers had spoken up forcefully about a possible catastrophic failure. Sometimes it's worth it to risk one's position by becoming a whistle blower. It was feared by some engineers that the heat shield on the shuttle was too weak for a safe re-entry, but the concerns were set aside. Apparently NASA personnel and government decision makers went into *groupthink* mode. The deaths of the astronauts on that mission have now become an often cited example of how *groupthink* works. *Groupthink* is a form of tunnel vision. Everyone feels obligated to accept the "right" point of view. Then they drift into one correct position, and if someone expresses a different point of view, it is likely considered as refusal to be a team player. Group members do not speak up. Illusions of invulnerability can easily set in, and with Columbia, the successful outcome they envisioned did not happen.

Church leaders are especially vulnerable to *groupthink*. Driven by a fixation on unity at all costs, they become cautious about saying what they really think. When I served on the board of a large church in San Jose, California, a skilled business leader who was board chairman refused to allow *groupthink* in our decision making. He asked individual members to candidly state their views, no matter how different those views might be from prevailing opinion. He asked board members to go on the record. No subjects or opinions were allowed to be left off the table for behind-the-back chatter outside the board meeting. For me, serving on a board under a leader who demanded transparency from each member, was highly enjoyable. The end result was a high level of true unity and an acceleration of productivity. This kind of authentic transparency is, sadly, the exception, not the rule. With an overriding desire for unity, obviously a worthwhile goal, church boards are good at creating illusions of unanimity while ducking the real thing. They do so in much the same way that magicians create illusions that only look real. For churches, such illusions eventually backfire.

In critical situations such as criminal trials, the failure or refusal of a witness to testify can send the innocent to prison and allow the guilty to go free. Such cowardly silence can wreck many lives. Whether it's fear of losing a job, desire for acceptance, or a misguided emphasis on unity, silence can be lethal.

Silence is valid and invaluable in many situations.

Silence is beneficial when conversations get out of control. This is especially true in close relationships between marriage partners, parents and children, and children and their siblings. One family counselor suggests that a workable plan for communication between spouses is to create specific, regular opportunities, such as every two or three weeks, to meet solely for the dual purpose to complement each other and to bring up items of dissatisfaction. It's very important, he says, to keep the ratio of compliments to faults high. He recommends doing this away from home, at some location that is not a favorite hangout. This kind of setting creates a neutral zone without interruptions – cell phones off, please. He urges taking turns telling each other what is pleasing in the relationship, praising each other's good qualities and thanking each other for specific favors. Then, he says, be open and honest in a gentle way about concerns and things bothering them. Then practice silence. He says walking or driving separately to the meeting place can help encourage such silence and the quiet reflection that goes with it. "It's OK to break the silence," he says, "with frequent *Thank Yous*."

Right timing in discipline is tied to effectiveness in child rearing.

To discipline a willfully disobedient five-year-old at 10:00 in the morning by telling him, "I'll tell your father when he comes home," is wrong timing. The child will have lost all connection between what he did that morning and the discipline he gets at 5:15 o'clock that afternoon. If the punishment is a "time out," the best time is immediately following the disobedience.

Right timing in war for victory.

In war, right timing is crucial. A Polish friend had parents who were young single adults just before World War II when the eastern part of Poland came under the control of the Soviet Union due to an infamous pact between Hitler and Stalin. He tells a fascinating story about the Nazi invasion of the Soviet Union. The Russians were entrenched on the eastern bank of the Bug River. The Germans carefully planned their surprise offensive from the western bank.

They attacked early Sunday morning when Russian soldiers were sleeping off their customary vodka hangover from Saturday night. When the Germans crossed the river, the Russians staggered out of their tents in their underwear and were slaughtered. The attack was timed perfectly for maximum surprise.

Right timing in one's broad life-cycle is as important as right timing in random situations.

Since *"there is a time to be born and a time to die,"* assuming an average life span, we must fit into this time frame all that we hope to accomplish. In some traditional societies where life stages of childhood, adulthood, marriage, child bearing, child-rearing, and grand-parenting are clearly defined, only minimal attention is required to address this issue. In some cultures, adolescence as we know it does not exist as a formal stage of life. Children go through rituals that transition them directly from childhood to adulthood. Historically, adolescence is a very recent category of life stages. In Western societies, however, with our high degree of individualism and with no clear cultural formula for addressing life stages, each person has to take responsibility to chart a course in life that is in harmony with biological reality. In this context, it is sadly easy to drift through life. To counteract that kind of spineless passivity, it is important early on in life to start casting visions of what you want for your future. Good timing requires proactive planning. One of my college professors challenged a class of us twenty-year-olds to think carefully about where we wanted to be in five, ten, fifteen and twenty years. "Write it down," he said. "Once a year revisit what you thought you wanted. Make adjustments as your goals change. Evaluate whether you are doing what it takes to reach your goal." Engineers might choose to put their long-range life goals in the form of a pert chart.

In terms of planning for a professional life, the consensus is that up to approximately age 35 it is best to focus on education, training, and work experience. When you approach 40, move into a leadership position and remain highly productive in such roles for years. Around age 60 or a bit beyond, pull back from the most demanding positions. This is the time to mentor younger leaders and to continue serving on boards of directors. The wisdom gained through the years of experience can be used for high level decision making and consultative guidance for the next generation. In one's older years, serving as a trusted advisor to younger persons is an honorable act of responsible life stewardship. *"Timely advice is lovely, like golden apples in a silver basket" (Proverbs 25:11).*

High expectations about life's seasons must be tempered by the reality of specific circumstances.

There is *"a time to mourn and a time to dance (Ecclesiastes 3:4).* This nugget of ancient wisdom fits a refugee relief trip to the Balkans I was on soon after the end of that region's civil war. On my flight to Bosnia from Vienna, Austria, I replayed in my mind the beautiful television scenes of the '84 Winter Olympics there. I remembered the images of spectacular scenery, the stories of three ethnic groups living together peacefully, and the portrayals of smiling visitors from all over the world enjoying their visits. As we approached Sarajevo from the air, the dramatic beauty of the mountains still beckoned and heightened my expectations. But once on the ground, the ruined rows of shattered buildings created a distorted collage of 3D devastation that was never intended for human beings. I listened to endless stories about that war's heartbreaking impact on the people of that region. The air was literally thick with sullen anger and inconsolable grief. This was a time to work through the terrible loss of life and the total loss of belongings, a time to repent of great evil done to good neighbors, a time to seek forgiveness that might take years, if ever, to give or receive. Yes, dancing there will have to wait perhaps for whole new generations to arrive.

By contrast, when communist rule collapsed in the Soviet bloc in the autumn of 1989, exuberant dancing broke out spontaneously all over Central Europe. The stunning fall of the Berlin Wall is imprinted in the minds of everyone who watched television news during those historic days. I was in Poland that early autumn and marveled at the happy faces I saw everywhere. They had already gained freedom. They could move about without being watched 24/7. Best of all, they could dance, freely, openly, joyously. And they did! This was truly one of the world's great moments of a *"time to dance."*

Life is filled with times of great contrast. All of the contrasting times described in *Ecclesiastes* are useful in honing your wisdom in discerning what time is the right time. When you look back on your life, you'll be glad and grateful that you kept *timing* at the center of all your decisions, actions, and communications. *When* and *what* are important questions to ask of all the decisions you make, the actions you take, and the words you communicate.

There is a time for everything, and a season for every activity under heaven: a time to be born and a time to die, a time to plant and a time to uproot, a time to kill and a time to heal, a time to tear down and a time to build, a time to weep and a time to laugh, a time to mourn and a time to dance, a time to scatter stones and a time to gather them, a time to embrace and a time to refrain, a time to search and a time to give up, a time to keep and a time to throw away, a time to tear and a time to mend, a time to be silent and a time to speak, a time to love and a time to hate, a time for war and a time for peace (Ecclesiastes 3:1-8).

Reflections:

1 - What contrasting times in this scripture especially relate to you? How do you plan to develop within your lifestyle better timing for decision making? Who is there to help you with developing such a plan?

2 - Give examples of timing that life itself controls and ones over which you have some or all control.

3 - In what ways does timing impact the decisions you are in the process of making? And what are the consequences?

CHAPTER 2
TURN LIFE'S DOWNSIDES INTO UPSIDES

"Meaningless! Meaningless!" says the Teacher. "Utterly meaningless! Everything is meaningless. What does man gain from all his labor at which he toils under the sun? Generations come and generations go, but the earth remains forever" (Ecclesiastes 1:2-4).

Nothing lasts.

"Everything is meaningless" can also be translated *"All is vanity." Ecclesiastes* starkly emphasizes the brevity of life. This Hebrew term for "brevity" calls up images of a fleeting breath or an evaporating vapor. The lesson here is that everything is temporary and on the verge of vanishing, especially our own lives.

We humans often link our sense of meaning to feelings of possession and permanence. This is a mistake of the first order. Everyone and everything has a life cycle, a beginning, an end, and a brief span of time in between. The key to making this universal limitation work for you is to embrace Solomon's complimentary insight that *"He (God) has made every-thing beautiful in its time" (Ecclesiastes 3:11).* All things beautiful – glorious sunsets, fields of tulips, performances of masterpieces – are framed in the context of fleeting impermanence, yet all are exquisitely beautiful and meaningful in their own present moment.

Therefore, engage what is right for each season of life. Childhood, youth, middle age, and old age all have built-in limitations, but they all have their own unique promises and possibilities.

Special events that mark the transitions to and from each phase of life are wonderful opportunities for maximum celebration. High school graduations, college commencements, new jobs, big promotions, birthdays, weddings, anniversaries, recitals, special accomplishments, even wakes, funerals, and memorial services all create occasions of happy celebration and serious reflection. Do not let these moments pass unnoticed or ignored. Capture the special highlights of the seasons of your life and the lives of those closest to you. Be creative about ways to make each phase of life *"beautiful in its time."*

Unique ways to do this.

One full year before my friend's mother turned 90, she contacted her two sisters and three brothers and said, "Since mother's favorite performer was Elvis, let's all get together and take her to Las Vegas for a concert by an Elvis impersonator." To make their mother's 90th a perfect family celebration, they and their spouses all agreed that only her six grown children would go with her. They rented a suite in a beautiful hotel suite decorated in their mom's favorite colors, blue and lavender. They all had their breakfasts together and set aside plenty of time to reminisce non-stop about their childhood – including dinner together. Then came the night of the performance. They made sure they had front-row seats. The Elvis "tribute artist," as they like to be called, made a point to single out the 90-year-old fan for special recognition to the audience. He publicly acknowledged her birthday, then did the show to her enormous delight. Could there be a moment more "beautiful in its time" than this, always to be remembered and relished forever?

Two years later at 92, the mother died. Yes, there were tears at her passing, but there was also great gratitude that they had all made such a special occasion for her 90th. All six children, their spouses, friends, and relatives gathered in the cemetery for the burial. There, a beloved family pastor read her favorite passages of Scripture and reflected on her deep faith in the promises of eternal life. But this story has an even more special finale. After the final prayer, the same Elvis tribute artist who had performed for her in Las Vegas suddenly appeared in full Elvis attire. In her honor, he sang three of her favorites: *Glory, Glory, and Hallelujah, The Green Green Grass of Home,* and *Hush Little Baby, Don't You Cry.* In that cemetery, time and eternity fused into one bright moment. Everyone present was crying and smiling at the same time. What a send-off. The Commandment to *"honor your father and your mother"* was kept in grand form that unforgettable day. Despite the sorrow of the final goodbye, the family's "beautiful moment" in their mother's honor memorably marked life's final transition.

It's always the right to do our part to *"make everything beautiful in its time."*

Life is endless repetition.

"Generations come and generations go, but the earth remains forever. The sun rises and the sun sets, and hurries back to where it rises. The wind blows to the south and turns to the north; round and round it goes, ever returning on its course. All streams flow into the sea, yet the sea is never full. To the place the streams come from, there they return again. All things are wearisome, more than one can say" *(Ecclesiastes 1:4-8).*

Repetition shows up in little ways. A guy walked into the gym and asked his friend working out next to me, "What's up?" After a brief silence, the reply was, "Same 'ole, same 'ole." Neither man registered any discontent with their state of affairs, probably because their lives were stable, and predictable. Apparently, without much thought, they had accepted repetition by adopting its upside.

Repetition makes predictability possible. Predictability, in turn, enables us to make plans for the future. In Denver, for example, heavy snows increase each year around the third week of January. That's when the moist air from the Gulf of Mexico starts to flow northward and collides with the frigid air of arctic cold fronts moving south. That's when you know you'd better have chains, blankets, a shovel, a few energy bars and some extra water in your vehicle, just in case you're caught in a blizzard. Then, when the frost lines move north and winter ends, gardeners know it's time to plant their vegetables.

When your son or daughter turns 13, you suddenly know in a mere 60 months you're going to have an 18-year-old high school graduate who is ready for work, college, or the military. Predictability gives us life's margin to get ready. So before you get bored by the so-called "same 'ole, same ole," remember to be thankful for repetition's built-in predictability about what's next.

Never enough.

"The eye never has enough of seeing, nor the ear its fill of hearing" (Ecclesiastes 1:8b).

So when is enough, enough? That's the question many grapple with about many things. Sometimes we win the battles, sometimes we lose. It's important to evaluate the issue of *enough* in your own lifestyle.

A young mother in Silicon Valley told me she dresses her children in clothes she buys at garage sales, often with items that still had price tags on them. A bit shocked, I asked, "Really?" She went on to say, "Yes, people just like to shop for their kids, but they never get around to using it all. They just keep on shopping and have way more than they need." She got the good out of their wasted money on the clothes they discarded.

In the matter of eating, a delightful young woman from Canada always seemed to eat very little on her plate, yet always seemed fully satisfied with her small portions, even of the most delicious servings. Whenever she was urged to enjoy a second helping, she had the most delightful reply. "Oh thank you, but no," she'd say in her clipped Canadian accent, "I've had plenty." She had a very keen sense of when for her enough was enough, and she was a healthy person for eating right.

Take the season ticket holder for symphony concerts at the Davis University of California Mondavi Center, who left in the middle of one dramatic performance. "When I went home at the intermission of a great concert," she confessed, "I knew then I had gone past *enough*." It was just too much of a very good thing.

What about guys who watch sports on weekends from morning till night, then watch the re-runs on weekdays? Sure, an occasional sports feast is fine, say during the World Series or the deciding games leading to the Super Bowl, or the key match ups leading to some college bowl or the best games of March Madness. But at some point, enough is truly enough. One person's observation hits home on this score. "Football is eleven guys down on the field desperately in need of rest and 70,000 people up in the stands and millions more on their sofas at home urgently in need of exercise."

Some people go overboard volunteering for everything that needs to be done at their church or civic club. It seems like a good thing to do, but is it? A line has to be drawn on even the most worthwhile activities. Ask yourself the question, "When does *therapeutic* become *toxic?*" Volunteering can be like medicines prescribed to relieve pain or facilitate a cure. Prescriptions that are taken in proper doses lead to better health, but if they are taken longer than prescribed or in excessive doses, debilitating toxicity, and sometimes death might occur. Volunteerism, like pain relieving Vicodin, can become addictive. A mature volunteer says "yes" part of the time, but may also say "no."

Individual and social problems of alcoholism, substance abuse, obesity, and gambling occur because early on the issue of *when is enough, enough* was not addressed. When I led a group of people who were discussing the matter of *enough* on Staten Island, NYC, a woman shared her past; "I ate so much and was so fat that I went to the beach one Sunday morning to kill myself. I hated my body. I hated life." Deciding at the last minute not to go through with her plan, she joined a church and *Overeaters Anonymous.* I would not have guessed that she struggled so.

While speaking in Las Vegas on W*hat's Important in Life* to participants in Alcoholics Anonymous, Gamblers Anonymous, Overeaters Anonymous, and Narcotics (AA, GA, OA, NA), a husband and wife in the GA group told me that they both lost their first marriages, their wealth (both had been well-to-do), and their professional positions because of uncontrolled gambling. "If I took hold of a slot machine," she said, "it was as though my hand was glued to it. I desperately wanted to let go, but couldn't. Now, I won't even walk through a casino." At last they were happily in control of their lives.

So when is enough of Justin Bieber, Rihanna, Lady Gaga, U2, Beethoven or Bach enough? How many tall mocha cafés with whipped cream? It seems that as Solomon reflected on nature and its endless cycle of unending appetites, he observed in himself and in others inclinations that mimic insatiable nature. Oceans are never full, even with the Nile, the Amazon, and the Mississippi Rivers flowing into them. So it is with the ear and eye, always wanting to download more music, attend more ball games, go to more night clubs, listen to more news, tune into more talk shows, shop for more stuff, acquire more things, make more money, pile up more degrees. Solomon had all the freedom, power, and resources at his command to do anything he wanted for as long as he wanted. But by reflecting on his own over-indulgences, he realized that even though he could have it all, there was never enough of whatever it was to truly satisfy him. We are *insatiable*. It requires mature, self-imposed limitations to be satisfied with *enough*. For some of us, these limitations may include the need to report or even confess to an accountability group or partner. But don't feel alone in this regard. With American society's endless options and enticements for over-indulgence in our 24/7 constantly connected life cycle, if you struggle with *enough,* you've got company galore.

What are the upsides of wanting more or something new? If the appetite for great food failed, you might not eat enough to stay alive. If the ear did not like different or new sounds, the world might fall silent. Or if the eye became satisfied, new generations of Rembrandts would not start painting. Very few might plan trips to be awed by Niagara Falls. And there would be little interest in New Year's Eve fireworks from Sydney to Stockholm.

It's normal to enlist desires to both survive and enrich life. Each human desire has a God-intended purpose! Focus energies there, on the proper use of desires, rather than allowing them to lead us astray. King Solomon was driven by natural desires to achieve great things in his kingdom. Some of the results of his efforts were beneficial, but after serious reflection, it became clear that all of the activity and achievement did not lead to fulfillment, and some of it was ultimately damaging to both him and his nation. Learn from his mistakes, and apply the brakes on *enough.* More will be said about Solomon's excesses in Chapter 5. One of his own proverbs might be applied to the management of his life: *"Like a city whose walls are broken down is a man who lacks self-control" (Proverbs 25:28).*

Knowledge, skill and wisdom fall short.

"I thought to myself, 'Look, I have grown and increased in wisdom more than anyone who has ruled over Jerusalem before me; I have experienced much of wisdom and knowledge.' Then I applied myself to the understanding of wisdom, and also of madness and folly, but I learned that this, too, is a chasing after the wind. For with much wisdom comes much sorrow; the more knowledge, the more grief (Ecclesiastes 1:16-18)."

King Solomon knew he exceeded all others in his grasp of diverse skills and his mastery of vast knowledge. But limitations beyond his control led him to declare that even though you may know what could be or ought to be, you often cannot make it happen. That's painful, and it happens all the time.

For example, musicians with excellent pitch silently suffer when a performer with a poor ear for intonation sings flat, but thinks he or she is right on pitch. How many embarrassing examples of this phenomenon have we witnessed on *American Idol?* Musicians will be exasperated by a costly new concert hall designed for visual appeal without proper attention to the all-important aspect of acoustics, leaving them unable to hear one another playing.

Good architects will be viscerally bothered by new buildings that lack balance, symmetry, unity, and elegant, intelligent, simple integration of form and function. My own father was an excavation contractor who was constantly incensed by the carelessness of novice or greedy builders who failed to plan for adequate drainage. When it rained on those residential sites, the surface water would flow straight into the garages. Anyone with special skills or knowledge in any field knows the frustration of seeing or dealing with things that fall far short of what they should be.

As new questions for managing life call for new answers, the cycle of dissatisfaction continues. But does this suggest that ignorance is bliss? Hold off on a yes. Solomon later wrote that it's better to know than not to know because you can at least see what's happening. He wrote, *"I saw that wisdom is better than folly, just as light is better than darkness. The wise man has eyes in his head, while the fool walks in the darkness; but I came to realize that the same fate overtakes them both" (Ecclesiastes 2:13, 14).* You can spot the pot holes in life and avoid them, at least some of them, if you have adequate information.

New social data and on-going scientific discoveries, when filtered through a sound value system and high ethical standards, can greatly help us have a better life. This is a true upside of the frustration.

The four downsides of life addressed in this chapter are universal. Others may be unique to your own life and situation, and they, too, will demand your attention. But you will find that many of them can be turned into upsides with a positive attitude and thoughtful, prayerful actions.

Reflections:

1 - Is there any area of your life in which you indulge beyond the point of "enough"? If so, how does this over-indulgence work against your efforts to live the "good life," and how will you correct the excess?

2 - Because nothing lasts, in the next six months, what opportunities do you foresee in your own life or in the lives of others close to you to "make things beautiful in their own time"?

3 - Life patterns for all of us have predictability. Which are feared, and which do you look forward to. How can you plan for that?

CHAPTER 3
ZERO IN ON LIFE'S BASICS

"Go, eat your food with gladness, and drink your wine with a joyful heart, for it is now that God favors what you do. Always be clothed in white, and always anoint your head with oil. Enjoy life with your wife, whom you love, all the days of this meaningless life that God has given you under the sun — all your meaningless days. For this is your lot in life and in your toilsome labor under the sun. Whatever your hands find to do, do it with all your might, for in the grave where you are going, there is neither working nor planning nor knowledge nor wisdom" (Ecclesiastes 9:7-10).

Enjoy your three meals, every day.

The high ratings of TV's Food Network show how much interest there is in enjoying food. My quick survey of the magazine shelves of *Barnes and Noble* showed more than fifty publications about food and beverages, plus at least one hundred books on food on the bargain table. There's no doubt about it, we have a love affair with food.

The French hold the trump card on food. Over the centuries, their enduring influence in their former colonies has always included their approach to food and the full enjoyment of life's simple pleasures. In the Middle East, for example, many of that region's finest chefs come from French-influenced Lebanon. I mentioned this to a Lebanese taxi driver in Phoenix,

Arizona. In full agreement, he laughingly replied, "We Lebanese *love* food. At breakfast, we talk about what we are going to have for lunch. At lunch, we talk about what we will have for dinner. At dinner, we talk about food again – what we are going to have for breakfast."

In Central Europe, it's Hungary that rivals the French for excellence in cuisine, which is why the Hungarians are often called "the French of Central Europe." They explain it this way: "We Hungarians focus on taste. The French focus on presentation." As for me, I'll take both.

California's Napa Valley sets some of the highest standards for food here in America. Restaurant owners from all over the nation regularly flock to the Napa Valley area to keep up on what's new on the food scene there. Whether it's a delectable lunch at the famed Culinary Institute of America (CIA) in St. Helena or a scrumptious sandwich at the V Sattui Winery European style deli and market, you can count on culinary perfection.

The wives of several of my friends specialize in preparing and enjoying special meals. It's always a pleasure to be in their homes for any celebration that includes food. Not that this should be a test of friendship, but it's a great experience every time it happens.

One of these families is Polish. For several years, I joined them for their Christmas Eve celebrations where every detail of the evening was planned exactly as it was in Poland before WWII. The grandmother, a teenager during that war, had been deported to Central Asia. But she courageously made her way to India, then Africa, the United Kingdom, then to Argentina, and finally to America. Here in 21st Century California, she faithfully kept Poland's traditional Christmas Eve celebration alive. When I told friends in Poland about these Christmas Eves in America, they questioned me about every detail. What I described to them matched exactly what they still do in Warsaw.

Another couple I know celebrates "Boxing Day," which comes from the upper class households of merry old England. On that day, December 26, the servants got to eat the leftovers from Christmas. Today it's a great way to have friends over for a post-Christmas party with traditional English food, including beef, potatoes, and cabbage slaw. Our hostess had carefully researched old English recipes, refined them, and threw great parties around that theme. Her beef rivaled the best of London or Buenos Aires. I'm positive no 19th Century Englishman ever tasted slaw as good as hers. I believe if the Queen of England herself had been there, she would have gone back for second servings of everything. The husband did his part by selecting fine wines from his ancestral homeland of Germany, plus picking just the right non-alcoholic drinks to match the menu. I confess, on those December 26th celebrations it took a special measure of self-control to know when *"enough was enough"* — and that limit was often exceeded.

A friend who is both nurse and an artist creates a special kind of enjoyment of food for others by her creative use of "color." The presentations of her meals are often as intensively vibrant in color as any outdoor fruit or vegetable market in the tropics. Some of her shades are as subtle as the delicate pastel hues of a Monet garden canvas. That's the artist part of her — and the taste always equals the art. Then the nurse in her character takes over. Her food is genuinely healthy.

No TV chef has anything on these hostesses. See for yourself, I've attached a recipe from each of them in an Appendix. It's also worth noting that some men star in "barbeque celebrations."

The chefs of France, Hungary, and Napa Valley have much to offer to our enjoyment of food. But the hostesses I've described often prove that the most exquisite food ever tasted and the most beautiful meals ever presented can come from our own kitchens. Also, make it a point to check with your own relatives about signature meals in your own family's history and heritage. You might be amazed at the recipes you'll uncover and the meals you savor — a grandmother's best lemon pie in the world, or a perfect wiener schnitzel.

In some countries it is the "outdoor" kitchens that rival the best restaurants. The tastiest lobster I've ever eaten was in the Philippines, cooked outdoors by our host. And the best tortillas? I found them in a rural area of Oaxaca, Mexico, made from freshly ground corn, baked over glowing charcoal, and served by the women while still warm. Sprinkled with a dash of salt, they were a stand-alone, Five-Star, welcoming appetizer for me and my friend, Roberto, as we arrived from Mexico City. I eagerly crossed the line of *enough* on those occasions, but excused myself on the handy rationale that there's a time to fast and a time to feast.

A few bits of advice about enjoying different kinds of food in far-away places: avoid anything that can't be peeled or isn't cooked. If it's fresh off the tree or just picked from the garden, it's usually OK. A proud gardener in a small village in the hills of Jamaica, showed his hospitality by pulling up a few carrots from his beautifully tended garden, scraping off most of the dirt, and handing each of us one to eat. We ate them right on the spot, residual dirt and all. They tasted wonderfully sweet, almost like nature's candy.

Oh yes, of course, never use ice cubes to cool a Coke or Pepsi. Learn to drink soda warm. Also, do not buy bottled water that isn't carbonated. Stick with carbonated mineral water. Experienced travelers can tell you all about the intestinal misery one can suffer by ignoring these guidelines.

Enjoy your clothes.

We have to wear clothes for the sake of modesty and protection from the elements. The writer of *Ecclesiastes* suggests, *"Dress in white and anoint your head with oil."* He may be saying, first, that we should not go around looking like an unmade bed. He may also be suggesting that we should dress up for celebratory occasions and that royalty should be regal in apparel and appearance. In the upscale hotels of the Middle East today, it is customary to see men at breakfast in ankle length traditional white attire as a sign of their wealth or royal status.

Like it or not, clothes make a definite statement about who we are. Whether our clothes are designer-made or off the rack, we can always present ourselves well dressed. During WWII, American women often wore "feed sack dresses." Hundred-pound sacks of animal feed were sold in a variety of print patterns. Women made dresses out of them, and they made shirts for the men. A friend from the rural Midwest said he and his brother wore "feed sack shirts" until their upper teens. They didn't get their "store bought shirts" until they got their driver's license. The war made fabric scarce, but people still found innovative ways to look good with what little they had to work with. Lowly feed sacks, it turns out, had a lot of potential for high fashion. It was a preview of today's ecological practice of creative recycling.

One single parent I know could barely make ends meet, but she always looked like the proverbial million dollars. I asked her how she did it. "Well," she said, "I go the best stores in town and try on a lot of their clothes to find out what's in fashion and what looks good. Then I go to *Goodwill* and find something like it for only a few dollars and alter it, if I need to." The result was that she never felt underdressed at work or in any social environment, because she always looked right in step with the latest styles.

David was described as "comely."

"Comely" is a term and a concept rarely used in modern times. It implies a man or a woman who by their appearance, dress, posture, and bearing, "looks to be a person of high quality or special importance." It's what we mean when we say of someone who presents himself well, "He looks like he really is somebody." The term was used in the Bible to describe the impressive, regal-looking King David, father of Solomon.

In our own time, whether it's how we dress for a job interview, work environment, social event, or informal time with friends and family, wearing appropriate, stylish clothes that fit the occasion helps us feel good about ourselves and also helps the people we are with feel more aware of their own significance in our presence.

Culture, of course, determines what is appropriate for various occasions, such as weddings, funerals, formal events, special celebrations, business environments, and weekend wear. What is acceptably casual in the beach town of Santa Monica, California, is totally different from what is considered properly casual in Washington, D.C. When engaging with other cultures it is vitally important in a global world to know what is considered to be modest. That standard varies considerably. It's a short flight from Milan, Italy to

Istanbul, Turkey, but what is modest in Italy is not modest in Turkey. Check local dress codes and respond accordingly.

Enjoy your spouse.

Be intentional about enjoying the most important person in your life. She is *first,* and some guys get it right. To them, it's second nature. "I take my wife to breakfast every Saturday morning I'm in town," is how one friend kept romance alive and communications flowing. When I asked a friend to lunch one Monday, he automatically replied, "That's my every-week lunch date with my wife. Can we make it on another day?" "Of course," as I thought, "lucky woman." Both men spent a lot of work time out of town, but they knew how to have a good marriage.

A 94-year old retired fireman from San Francisco, who worked out at gym every morning, took his wife dancing every Friday night. And on mornings she didn't feel like working out, she still came to the gym with him and while she waited for him, drank coffee in the gym lobby. I lost track of them when they moved to be near their 72-year old son, just in case they eventually needed help! These three men had "standing dates." They knew their priorities. A lot of us, when in our 20s can barely earn a "C" in *Wife Enjoyment 101.* It gets better with some well-guided effort.

Seize every moment of possible enjoyment with your husband or wife. Five days before my wife's sudden and untimely death, as we were talking about the kids and work, I said, "You are an exceptional person, and I don't say that because you are my wife and the mother of our children. You really are exceptional." She smiled and said that Eileen, her colleague in the music department said the same thing over lunch a few days before. My feelings captured in words that evening appeared to be more satisfying than those of her fellow instructor. I was just enjoying my wife. And little did I know that this would be the last week I would ever have the opportunity to share my feeling about her, with her.

The *Song of Solomon,* the book right after *Ecclesiastes,* focuses on a spouse's physical attributes.

God created, endorsed, and promotes sexual relations in marriage. In this six-page poetic book, a young man says, *"How beautiful you are, my beloved..."* She responds, *"What a lovely pleasant sight you are, my love..." (Song of Solomon 1:15, 16).* This is only a starter. You might want to take a few minutes to read the rest of the book.

Enjoying your spouse goes beyond physical attraction.

The strength, skills, and dignity of a woman fit to be a queen are featured in *Proverbs 31,* another Wisdom Literature book. Her husband would appreciate her compassion to do good for others and skill in dealing with finances and the complexity of household management.

Will spouses enjoy each other every day of married life?

Realistically, not likely. That's why pre-marital counselors raise the question of how you handle anger. One day, you may be surprised that you are mad at your wife. When anger surfaces, it's necessary to acknowledge it, and calmly explain what caused the frustration or hurt. Anger is an alert that something is wrong, but if the anger is too intense to address the issue immediately, be honest and say, "I'm too upset to talk about it right now. Let's talk tomorrow." The key to resolving the problem, and not allowing it to fester, is to follow through with the commitment. Caution! By the next morning the intensity of the anger may have subsided, and talking through the issue as promised may be ignored. That can lead to deterioration in the relationship. Pledge to each other that you will talk about this when cool enough to be constructive. Verbalize, "I love you and want to resolve this." Keep in mind that men are likely to cool off and then the problem becomes a non-issue. Because we males tend to compartmentalize life and issues, when we no longer feel heated, an issue feels resolved. What is forgotten by men because the issue seems to be resolved is likely to be remembered by women. Therefore, it is important to talk out a problem until its implications are fully understood and a way forward is agreed upon.

What if boredom creeps into your marriage?

If you wake up some morning after 15 years of marriage wondering what you saw attractive in your husband or wife, it may be that gradually you drifted apart. Every ounce of energy went to career development and child rearing. It's time to go to counseling. Life situations change. Spouses change during a long marriage. A lecturer over 70 said, "My wife has been married to five different men, and they have all been me." Major life transitions such as retirement, moving into a new community, coping with teenagers, both husband and wife finding themselves unemployed, and serious health issues are best dealt with by seeking professional counseling. One of the most demanding transitions occurs when one spouse changes religion or decides to become an atheist while the other person continues to believe. In reviewing transitions, the first major transition was when the first son or daughter was born. Both parents lost 700 hours of sleep the first year. What an adjustment! Life changed. And life keeps changing.

Intentional time together can be forgotten in any marriage as time goes by. And "intentional" is the key to keeping a relationship alive. Sometimes, when all of the children have left home, a husband and wife may begin to focus on separate deferred goals and interests. But they were just waiting until the children were reared. That's a setup for drifting apart. In Chapter 10, dealing with what's important for youth, I mention how a high school music teacher and his wife ignited my adventurous spirit. When school was out, they went to Canada every summer for camping and fishing on remote lakes. In his own words, "When the last of our six kids left home, we looked at each other and asked, 'What do we do now?' That's when we got the idea of doing something we both loved. After tossing around ideas, we couldn't think of anything more fun, quiet, and peaceful than having a canoe on a lake in the North Woods of Canada. And the canoe had to be red."

To sustain mutual appreciation of each other, on wedding anniversaries take a bit of time to backtrack down memory's lane and review what you found appealing when you first met and dated. Good memories are like old photos. It might rekindle feelings of early romance.

Marital enjoyment takes an investment of time, energy, and isolation. That may mean cutting out some activities and limiting the number of other people in your life, or the impact they have on your marriage. Marriage is a private retreat. *"You are a garden locked up, my sister, my bride; you are a spring enclosed, a sealed fountain" (Song of Solomon 4:12).* Appreciation of each other, combined with love and respect and enough time alone, just the two of you, go a long way to sustaining a happy marriage.

If single, you may be asking how this section on enjoying your spouse can speak to you.

Having been married, though single now, my thoughts on that are if you have children, nieces, nephews, or married friends, it's good to be familiar with basics about a good marriage. You might be called upon to share this kind of information with family members and friends. I know there is no substitute for a spouse and the intimacy of marriage, but a full social life with both men and women, couples and other singles, can go a long way in addressing loneliness and the vulnerability of being alone. In singles conferences where I have spoken, it appears that those who manage being single the best are involved in organized groups. Some churches sponsor special events for singles' interests by age, financial ability, and the right kind of activities for both those with and without children. As singles engage in co-ed activities, they occasionally meet someone who turns out to be a good mate!

For athletic types, kayak or fishing clubs insure recreational activities with others, and I've noticed that handball buddies, if single, are always going to find a way of not being alone on Independence or Labor Day.

Volunteering for community service projects also builds satisfying relationships. One widow who had the leisure and means went to a children's hospital in Palo Alto, California and painted the nails of little girls being treated for cancer or other diseases. The girls loved it, and felt beautiful. Sometimes she served as a volunteer for a county suicide hot line. She was never uncertain about having wonderful friends and was invited to more social events than she could possibly attend.

Holidays can be a problem.

Think creatively. Two single women who became acquainted in their church group, each a parent with one daughter the same age and with no extended family nearby, decided to launch a new Christmas tradition. On Christmas Eve they got together for a light meal and games, followed by a sleepover. Christmas Day started with coffee and traditional German marzipanstollen. Pancakes for the girls. And a gift exchange. Finally, in the afternoon, an old fashioned Christmas dinner. This tradition lasted until the girls were almost grown.

Single parents with children do well to have couples as friends.

Their children have the opportunity to observe how husbands and wives interact with each other, an understanding hard to come by in a single-parent home.

When singles entertain couples, it's usually better to invite two couples rather than just one because that insures a ratio of two men to three women or three men to two women, and most people are more comfortable socially with this mix. In a book I'm writing on how to manage single life, I plan to address this issue fully.

Marriage is the first institution created by God, foundational to every well-functioning society. It is intended to contribute to our stability, personal happiness, and a good life, even when life is rough.

Enjoy your work.

Single or married, another basic fact of life for most of us is the significant amount of our time we must spend in our occupations. Solomon wrote, "Whatever your hand finds to do, do it with all your might *(Ecclesiastes 9:10)*. *"Lazy hands make a poor man, but diligent hands bring wealth... As vinegar to the teeth and smoke to the eyes, so is a sluggard to those who send him"* *(Proverbs 10:4, 26)*.

When Jim took his first job selling shoes, an older friend said to him, "From now on you are going to be spending most of your time working. You will do yourself a favor to discover what makes your work enjoyable." Jim took that advice. He began to study feet. He learned the many kinds of problems people have with their feet and the kinds of shoes that help ease or solve those problems. He became a respected expert on the right styles of shoes and attire for different occasions. He could carry on a full evening of fascinating conversation about people, outfits, events, and shoes.

Work has spiritual purpose.

The Bible links work and worship so closely that work is seen as an expression of worship – part of the reverent service we gratefully render to God, not some drudgery that we grudgingly render to men. This linkage of work with worship lifts it far above the mere humdrum level of routine to a place of high honor. In the *Genesis* account of creation, God gives Adam and Eve the task of tending the Garden of Eden. God commissioned them to join Him in gardening activity and not leave it *au natural.* Once they were forced to leave the garden with the entrance barred behind them, work took on all the odious aspects that have burdened man ever since. We all experience the weariness of work just as people did when *Ecclesiastes* was written. But despite that tedious reality, *Ecclesiastes* declares that work can still be personally meaningful, deeply therapeutic, and highly beneficial for both one's self and one's community.

To enjoy work is obviously more daunting for people who live under oppressive governments, with all their arbitrary, bureaucratic rules and strict regulations on the kind of work that individuals or groups can do based on such artificial restrictions as age, race, and gender. People trapped behind the Communist Iron Curtain in Europe faced exactly that kind of difficult situation. Political loyalty rather than personal competence determined who got what job, thus stifling and stunting the energy and aspirations of the larger population.

One of the saddest comments about work and workers I heard early on during the post-Communist era was on a visit to the stunningly beautiful Prague Castle in the Czech Republic. As I stood next to the castle wall looking over the city, I asked a man nearby, who looked Slavic, if he was from Russia. "No," he said, "I'm Czech and I teach in California. Just back here for a visit." He said it was his first visit since the fall of the communist system there. He then mused aloud, "Where are all the intelligent faces? I remember how bright and smart the people were before the Communist era. But I guess when you've once been a university professor and then are forced by the government to work for years digging in the mines or driving a street car, your face slowly goes blank."

I've listened to many such stories in my travels in Central and Eastern Europe. I confess I don't have a lot of advice for people in such situations. Enjoyment of one's work sometimes has to be downgraded to merely filling the hours of the day to survive. That's all that can be expected in those systems. But even in such dire circumstances, the work involved in managing one's home or preparing food or helping others with tasks apart from one's regular work are alternative places to look for personal fulfillment and express individual creativity. I saw fleeting touches of this kind of fulfillment in Romania where nationals entertained me in their homes after our clandestine teaching sessions. Even though they were under the heavy pressure of breaking the law that forbid them to have any contact with Westerners, they clearly took great delight in creatively preparing and graciously serving what little food they had to share.

Immigrants face job barriers.

It's often hard for immigrants or refugees to find work they truly enjoy. I once bought a car from a highly educated North African engineer. He was a political refugee who was selling Fords until he could work his way into a more fulfilling job and become a US citizen. Even though he seemed thoroughly engaged in his work, as we talked about his past in Africa and his potential in America, it was clear that he had goals far beyond selling cars. Many, like him, do whatever they must to get started, but also take steps to be certified in whatever profession or occupation they want to work at. They also focus on becoming proficient in English.

Developing new skills enhances enjoyment.

In an open society where you can make your own choices about work, the basic reality is that you must develop skills that are necessary to excel in what you want to do. Competence is the key to both success and enjoyment in whatever work you choose. To achieve this kind of career excellence you must know both your gifts and your limitations, those that are permanent and those that are only temporary. To achieve this kind of personal growth, you must always be willing to push beyond your current comfort levels into areas that challenge you and activities that stretch you.

Attitudes toward work are changing.

Over the last few generations, the goal of enjoying one's work by providing quality products and excellent services has given way to seeking enjoyment as a shopper and consumer. Work ends up being only a way to buy things or experiences. The value of work for its own sake is greatly diminished and becomes burdensome. A shift back to our earlier attitudes would, in my view, yield far more meaning to all the work we do.

A story is told that might help turn us back in a more positive direction. A Greek sculptor was working meticulously on the hair on the back of the head of a marble statue. A bystander asked, "Why are you being so careful working on the back of the statue's head? No one will ever see it." The sculptor replied, "The gods will see it." The desire to work to win God's approval for one's attitudes and efforts is a powerful motivational force.

Solomon occasionally illustrated the points he wanted to make about human behavior by using examples of animal activity and habits. A modern application of this approach for urging people to enjoy their work could come from the story of Bodie, a K-9 partner on the Sacramento police force. Bodie was shot while chasing a criminal, and though he recovered, he could not leap over high fences. He wanted to continue patrol duty and whined as his handler left for work each day. Bodie was issued a reserve K-9 badge and assigned to the new task of training his successor. Bodie's story serves as a model of loving work and finding new, though more limited, labor when circumstances force us to abandon former roles.

Stay focused on the basics.

The happiest people I know are those who have discovered that investing time and energy in the simple, basic, ordinary things is the best way to achieve and enjoy a truly good life.

Scripture says that all that is good and perfect comes from God above. Spouses, children, extended family, work, food, clothing are all among His many gifts to us. He has given us these gifts and ultimately, it is attention to the basics I have described in this chapter that bring us the most personal happiness.

Most of us need to work for income. It also takes work just to do the routine activities that keep our daily lives pulled together – shopping, cooking, washing clothes, ironing, cleaning the house and having the car serviced. So it's worth the effort to find ways to enjoy whatever our work and tasks may be. Also, since the majority of us are married or would like to be married, learning how to appreciate our spouses and family and how to give them special attention can yield great mutual satisfaction. And we all eat. To enhance our enjoyment of one of life's necessities, let's adopt some of the creative approaches to food of the French, Hungarians, Lebanese, and denizens of Napa Valley, even if it's just at the evening dinner table with family and friends. Finally, let's pay attention to look our best – to look like we're *somebody*. *Ecclesiastes* gives us the guidelines for the fullest enjoyment of these gifts.

Reflections:

1 - How do your efforts for enjoyment of life align with the areas of focus in *Ecclesiastes,* such as, how much money is spent that enhances enjoyment without being destructive?

2 - Are you able to enjoy your food in a healthy way without feeling resentment? Why or why not?

3 - In your work, how do you manage non-stop technological changes and advancements?

CHAPTER 4
THERE'S MORE TO LIFE THAN WORK

"There was a man all alone; he had no brother. There was no end to his toil, yet his eyes were not content with his wealth. 'For whom am I toiling," he asked, *"and why am I depriving myself of enjoyment?"... Two are better than one, because they have a good return for their work: If one falls down, his friend can help him up. But pity the man who falls and has no one to help him up! ... Though one may be overpowered, two can defend themselves. A cord of three strands is not quickly broken"* (Ecclesiastes 4:7-12).

Balance work, relationships, and the rest of life.

In our 24/7 world, the art of balancing relationships and work is tricky. A good starting point in the quest for this balance is a well-defined set of values. What you truly believe about the importance of balancing your work and your relationships is the first key to your success or failure in achieving that balance. The second key is the determination and self-discipline you bring to putting into practice what you believe. Keeping your balance between work and relationships is as important as keeping balance exercises in your workouts at the gym. In both contexts you can learn skills to improve your balance. At the gym you can practice standing on one leg while doing bicep curls. At work and home, you can practice refining your daily schedule and improving your use of time.

The fact that friendships are so important to achieving and enjoying a good life should motivate you to give high priority to your relationships. Friendships are a strong protection against fragile feelings of personal vulnerability. Lebanese philosopher Khalil Gibran put it simply, "A friend is your needs answered." In Lebanon and other Middle East cultures, friendships form the core of their value systems. Similar value systems have stood the test of time everywhere.

If the large number of positive biblical references about "one another" is telling us something important about life, then you should never ignore the vital importance of initiating and maintaining strong relationships. If you habitually have no time for others, it's time to revisit your core value system and reevaluate how you are spending your time.

Friendships that last grow like trees. New growth rings develop year after year as the tree grows taller and its roots go deeper. In village settings, such friendships develop naturally. The principle holds true both in the tight-knit urban neighborhoods of Boston that Herbert J. Gans described in his famous 1962 book, *The Urban Villagers,* and equally in small towns like Holyoke, Colorado, where my late wife grew up. People in these settings know each other well, share a common culture, and always know when anyone has a need. They respond quickly. Everyone thinks of himself as a "first responder." The downside of village life is loss of privacy. It's been said that no surveillance system in the world is more effective than a small town.

I got a first-hand glimpse of an East Coast urban village on a hot, humid, 95-degree day in the New York City borough of Brooklyn in 1968. I was there helping lead college students in a summer social service internship. We dropped into a neighborhood grocery store for sodas just in time to overhear a regular customer say to the grocer, "My alarm clock isn't working. I got up too late this morning." The grocer replied, "You should have let me know. I would have phoned you." That was a village society in action.

I discovered the same village values in Vienna, Austria, a decade later. An Austrian couple with a new baby lived across the hall in our apartment building. They were both engineers. They gladly put their skills to neighborly use by showing me how to operate my Italian-made washing machine, which was very different from my Sears Kenmore back in California. One floor above me, a skilled musician in the Vienna Philharmonic practiced beautiful scores of classical music. It made for easy listening as I worked in my study.

All eight families in my building kept skis, boots and other extra household items in the *keller*, the street level storage room to which we each had a key. My belongings were stored in an area with a neighbor's items next to mine. There was no locked separation between us. We all trusted one another. Nothing was ever stolen, not so much as a ski glove. We all shopped at the same nearby shops, and we always spoke with neighbors from other nearby apartment buildings. My neighbors would offer friendly corrections to my *German*, as needed. One day at the fruit market, I asked for five apples using the *singular* noun. The woman waiting on me held up two apples and said *nein*, shaking her head *no* as she repeated the *German* terms I had used. Then she pointed to the two apples and used the plural. I made my request again, correctly this time, and we both smiled. I have never forgotten the plural *German* form of *apple*. Most important, I found village life in that grand international city to be very satisfying.

However, in most urban and suburban settings, a community of friends has to be crafted intentionally, based on common interests. An easy way to forge new friendships is by joining groups or participating in a variety of community activities. Friendships naturally develop as people interact and become better acquainted. However, it is wise to use great caution about seeking or forming deep relationships in the workplace. If personal conflicts or dissatisfactions between you flare up, it becomes extremely difficult to separate personal relationships from professional responsibilities. Failure to keep personal feelings from affecting one's job performance could cost one or both parties their jobs.

On the Peninsula south of San Francisco, four husbands and their wives became acquainted while working in similar industries and community service projects. They discovered they all shared a common interest in creating exciting dinner menus. That led to rotating monthly dinners, with one couple planning the menu and hosting the dinner each month. Over time, their relationships deepened. They were always available for one another if a need arose. Those close bonds, though tested, held firm when one of the men suddenly died. Even with a beloved member missing, those monthly dinners continued for many years and were a great source of strength and comfort for the surviving widow. The Scripture was proven true: *"There is a friend who sticks closer than a brother"* *(Proverbs 18:24).*

Without a circle of friends, single adults are very vulnerable.

Singles should have a core support group of three to five people to call if an emergency occurs. It is wonderfully assuring to know you have friends who will be there for you to provide both emotional and physical help, if needed. A single-again mother facing the possibility of homelessness was assured by a slightly older married couple, "If you ever have a month that you can't pay your rent, let us know. We'll cover you." She was so glad to know she suddenly had a safety net, and she was so grateful she never had to use it, although some months she was right on the edge.

Fun together is better than fun alone.

One day in a small coastal town in Italy, I watched several old men play *bocce*, a lawn-bowling game. I would wager those aging fellows had been playing together since boyhood. The great enjoyment they exuded just being together was contagious. They radiated such a happy aura of inclusion that it swept in everyone nearby. I was a foreigner who didn't even know the language, just sitting there for a snack and drink. But I felt as if I truly belonged in their company.

In a very different environment, two widows in Silicon Valley became acquainted through volunteer work with an arts organization and quickly discovered they had other common interests. They decided to occasionally spend a weekend in Napa Valley to relax, enjoy fine food, and take in the made-for-movies scenery. They would drive up together and then go *dutch*, each with her own room and breakfast schedule. Later in the morning they would peruse stores together, then enjoy a light lunch and a bit later drop into an inviting coffee shop. In the evenings, they would enjoy an elegant dinner in one of that area's great restaurants. Their backgrounds were very different, one a scientist who had defected from a Central European country controlled by communism, the other a native Californian who grew up in the Sierra foothills, then lived in East Coast cities for several years. Both loved the arts, cooked exquisite meals, and had several other friends in common. Their experience is a prime example that a network of diverse friends with shared interests opens doors for a rich variety of activities that add great value and enjoyment of life.

Guys often get together to play ball. When I lived in Cupertino, on an early Sunday morning walk with my dog past the junior high school, I watched weekend athletes playing soccer, communicating in *Spanish*. At the same playground later in the day, *Russian* was the language of those soccer games. Both groups were having fun. Playing a sport they grew up with and communicating in their "mother tongues" made it easy to develop and sustain friendships in a multi-ethnic suburban community. On Sundays they did not feel like outsiders. I know that feeling. If you've ever lived in a foreign culture, as I have, you know how satisfying it is, even if only a few times a month, to enjoy what is familiar to you and forget about adapting to new ways of thinking, speaking and doing things.

An easy way to make friends is to take advantage of a region's special days.

One couple enhances friendships by hosting Memorial Day patio brunches, with everyone chipping in on the menu. A Labor Day hike in a state park is great for any adventurous, able bodied group. Seize *St. Patrick's Day* or *Cinco de Mayo* for a dinner party. Highlight those dates with new twists on ethnic dishes and flashy table decorations. Keep it simple and fun. Forget "elaborate," unless it's your big fling of the year.

Work is important.

"The fool folds his hands and ruins himself" (Ecclesiastes 4:5). It takes food, clothing, housing, medical care, and transportation to live. The book of *Proverbs* reinforces what *Ecclesiastes* says about the value of work to provide for these basics, with sharply worded statements that zero in on the negative consequences of laziness. *"One who is slack in his work is brother to one who destroys"* (Proverbs 18:9). Laziness destroys things in the same way that arson burns down a house or a vandal slashes a priceless painting or a malicious bully spreads lies on social media to mutilate someone's reputation. That's how bad laziness is. *"Laziness brings on deep sleep, and the shiftless man goes hungry"* (Proverbs 19:15). The *New Testament* takes this insight a step further. A key principle of the benevolence of the early church was, *"If a man will not work, he shall not eat"* (Thessalonians 3:10). *"The sluggard craves and gets nothing, but the desires of the diligent are fully satisfied"* (Proverbs 13:4). This is just how life works. Smart people get with the program. The will and discipline to work hard increases income and builds wealth. That's an enduring life principle, valid in every era.

The Bible's view of work is so closely linked to worship that one might rightly ask, "Is work worship?"

Both words come from the same Hebrew root, *advodah,* meaning "to serve." Throughout the Bible, from God's work in creation to the Apostle Paul's letter to early Christians, work is always seen as worthy of honor and respect. The belief that *worship* is limited to what takes place inside a designated building restricts the full concept of *worship.* I believe Mother Teresa was worshipping God every time she fed the hungry, cared for the sick, and comforted the dying in the streets of Calcutta. Those who currently bring relief to victims of wars, famines, and earth-quakes can rightly see their work for their fellow man as authentic acts of *worshipping* God. Abraham Lincoln said it well, "The debts we owe to God are payable to our fellow man."

All kinds of work, from manufacturing automobiles, performing complex surgeries, to growing wheat, done as fulfillment of God's mandate to work, is *worship.*

What is the right amount of work?

Once we realize the importance of work, the question is, "How much work is right in relationship to the rest of life? The answer will be different for different people, but most societies come up with some basic guidelines that fit their cultures. However, it will be your responsibility and your challenge to figure out how much is right for you. In defense of hard work, someone quipped, "All work makes Jack a dull boy, but all work makes *jack*!" That is often the truth, but that is also the dilemma. In a marriage, two full-time wage earners have more money than when only one is employed, but less time for each other. Or one person with several jobs, one full-time and another part-time, has more money to spend, but less time for friendships. The choice is often more things or more time with others.

My father struggled with overdoing the work side of the work/relationship equation. He came of age during the Great Depression and worked hard driving a truck for the Works Progress Administration (WPA). He then developed his own business in that devastated economy. He loved work and he was disgusted at lazy employees, but he struggled to know when to put the brakes on his work. This dilemma is common for people who run their own businesses. Owning a business often means the business owns you. My father regularly worked 55 – 60 hours a week. But he finally concluded, "You can make as much money in six days a week as you can in seven." Take a sabbath.

If excessive work had not always been a possibility, it would not have been mentioned in *Ecclesiastes* nearly three thousand years ago. The danger of too much work is especially strong in our industrialized and post-industrial societies, with accelerating globalization. It is necessary at times to simply pull the plug on your 24/7 connectivity and availability to bosses, clients, and customers.

What happens when too much work throws our lives too far out of balance?

Capable and productive employees may walk away from their positions, saying, "Enough of this is enough." Companies are hurt when key people leave. A former vice president of a prominent high tech company, who left a lucrative and powerful position, says, "Every time I look up and see a plane overhead, I'm glad I don't have to be on it."

Couples drift apart. Neglected spouses are sitting ducks for meeting someone else who takes time to affirm them and enjoy their company. Then comes the breakup of the marriage. In marriages that survive overwork, one or both spouses may be so exhausted that their relationship goes flat. Their once vividly colorful love turns to a dull shade of gray. Then they make the situation worse by throwing themselves into even more work or going off to do their own things, thinking that will solve the problem. He goes duck hunting with his buddies; she goes to yoga class, or both to other diversions. Neglected sons and daughters are left with no positive model of marriage to follow and no helpful parental guidance about the struggles they are having or the questions they are asking. They have no clear limits about their behavior and little non-sexual affirmation of their personal value. This is the perfect set up for unwholesome and even criminal behaviors to creep into their lives.

Emergencies arise that force people to overwork to survive.

A family with five children faced the terrible news that one daughter had cancer and needed their special care. Their medical bills were sky high. Their other four children still had to be cared for. The parents bravely buckled down, worked harder and longer than ever, and dispensed with any kind of normal life. Their long ordeal eventually ended. Their daughter was well again, and they took deliberate steps to return to a balanced life – steps that some people fail to take. It's easy to get stuck in survival mode and keep on practicing the excesses that need to go in the waste bin.

Military service and work abroad can demand long periods away from home.

On a layover in a European airport, I met a man from the U.K. who was headed off for two months to the southern region of the former Soviet Union to super-vise workers in the petroleum industry. His routine was to work there for two months and return home for one month. Since I had taught in Eastern Europe on family issues, I asked a sensitive question about the morality of the workers. He casually responded that there are plenty of prostitutes available and some of the men, married or not, use their services. He said his workers didn't understand his faithfulness to his wife. I asked how his wife dealt with his long absences. "When I'm home," he said, "I spend all of my time with her. I take her on trips to Brazil and other places. We really make the most of our time together." This arrangement would not work for everyone, but they had managed to create an acceptable balance in their situation.

Burnout is often the result of long-term overwork.

People who are especially vulnerable to burn-out or compassion fatigue include social workers, teachers, doctors, family counselors, mental health specialists, who often have heavy loads of very troubled clients, plus law enforcement officers in high stress environments, and good-hearted volunteers who are constantly involved in demanding projects. Their noble desire to help others leads them into believing they can and must save the world around them. But at some point, the vortex of overwork leaves them drained and their ability to help greatly diminished. Some grow cynical about life in general and disillusioned about how much good, if any, they are doing. That's when social withdrawal becomes part of the picture, and chronic irritability leads to poor judgment and faulty decisions.

Overdoing a good thing, whether as a professional or as a volunteer, has a high price – burnout and prolonged periods of depression. The negative impact on lives is sometimes permanent.

Physical stresses associated with overwork, even where burnout does not occur, can still lead to ill health. A well-documented correlation exists between work and early death. The mind and the body are put under more pressure than they can sustain, even as their strong will keeps trying to push through with the work load.

The Japanese are well known for their diligent work habits. They have developed a theory called *karoshi,* which means *"death by overwork." Karoshi* is officially reported in its own separate category as a cause of death, even though it is often problematic to prove this syndrome as the cause of death.

In China, suicide rates increase dramatically among people who move from rural areas with strong family ties and community support to urban jobs and crowded apartment buildings. The problem is so serious that some apartment buildings have put nets at low levels to catch those who jump from upper floors. Overwork is certainly not the only reason a person decides to commit suicide, but excessive hours of work and poor working conditions can lead to depression and giving up on life. Death may seem the only way out of a hopeless rut.

Groups still exist where the concept of *work* as we know it is absent and unknown.

A few isolated tribes in the Amazon are still hunters and gatherers. The men hunt wild game, the women gather food from the forest and do the cooking. That's the limit of their *work,* other than making simple shelters for protection from the rain and small coverings for their bodies, if they wear anything at all. Their work is only for simple survival, no currency needed. But as urbanization and globalization spread, more and more of the world's population will be drawn into work as we know it. The need to balance work and relationships will need regular attention, in the media for public awareness and in official recognition for public policy.

In modern societies, when dealing with overwork at the personal level, engagement in small group discussions and one-on-one conversations, buttressed by mentoring and counseling, can go far in helping us gain better balance between our work, our relationships, and the other parts of life.

History can give us a helping hand.

When *Ecclesiastes* was written, the concept of the beginning and ending of a day was the opposite of 21st Century calendars and clocks. Each new day began at sundown. Therefore each day started with *rest,* and the second part of the day was for *work,* after *rest*oration and after breakfast. Today we function as though the day begins at sunrise. The ancient Sabbath Day was dedicated to rest, with no cooking, dishwashing, house repairs, or travel. The Sabbath began at sundown of the seventh day of each week, our Friday evening, and lasted to sundown on Saturday evening. This means those who kept the Sabbath had two consecutive nights of rest before the six-day work cycle. This down-time gave a structured, built-in time to nurture and enjoy relationships. It provided regular rest days that minimized the possibility of *karoshi* or burnout. Without such culture-wide time-structuring in our modern societies, we're on our own to figure out how to keep our work and the rest of our life in balance. Those who work at it with self-discipline do succeed, but we have to be intentional about it.

Good management of life includes adequate time for rest and adequate energy for work. Both are essential for a full life. Other people need us, and we need them. The Scriptures give clear guidance about our involvement with others. Jesus said, *"A new command I give you: Love one another. As I have loved you, so you must love one another"* (John 13:34). The Apostle Paul said, *"Be completely humble and gentle; be patient, bearing with one another in love"* (Ephesians 4:2). *"Be kind and compassionate to one another, forgiving each other, just as in Christ God forgave you"* (Ephesians 4:32). *"Therefore encourage one another and build each other up, just as in fact you are doing... Help the weak, be patient with everyone...*

Make sure that nobody pays back wrong for wrong, but always try to be kind to each other and to everyone else"
(1 Thessalonians 5:11-15).

I knew a family in Denver with a five-year-old who had been diagnosed with diabetes. An older couple living nearby knew a young family in Kansas City who also had a five-year-old diabetic child. They called that family in Kansas City and invited them to bring that child for a visit. They then arranged for the two children to eat together so that the newly diagnosed child could be helped in adjusting to a diabetic diet and its regulated eating schedule. This act of unique kindness set the bar high for the rest of us.

In our age of information bombardment and social networking, a final word of caution.

It is vital to create contexts for relationships to flourish. This includes eliminating the distraction of always keeping one eye on the smart phone when having coffee or lunch with a friend. Put the phones out of sight. Without giving our undivided interest to others, we will never get beyond superficial relationships. Do your texting at work if that's part of your job or in solitude, but not when you're engaged with others. To keep life enjoyable, commit both to your work and to one another, then organize your schedule to follow through with that commitment. You will be glad you did. Life satisfaction will be yours.

Reflections:

1 - Of the people you know, what examples of involvement with others are worthy of emulation? Are you willing to ask those key people into your life and learn what and how they think?

2 - Does your monthly calendar schedule match your intentions to balance relationships and work?

3 - How would you apply the following declaration and assertion: *Work* is *wor*ship, but do not *wor*ship *wor*k? Note *Colossians 3:23: "Whatever you do, work at it with all your heart, as working for the Lord, not for men."*

CHAPTER 5
SET LIMITS ON PLEASURE FOR THE GREATEST HAPPINESS

"I denied myself nothing my eyes desired; I refused my heart no pleasure... yet when I surveyed all that my hands had done and what I had toiled to achieve, everything was meaningless..." (Ecclesiastes 2:10-11).

Pleasure is seductive.

"For flowers and music I have lived," quipped my college piano teacher as we entered his iris garden for a break from a demanding lesson on the *Verdi/Liszt Rigoletto Paraphrase* for an upcoming recital. The garden was filled with vivid colors of lavender, purple, and yellow. With a cigarette in one hand, he proudly pointed out his favorite blossoms with child-like excitement. While he focused on flowers and music, his wife concentrated on elegant food. He often praised her culinary skills. She was also the one who chose the perfect art pieces for their home brought back from trips to Europe. So in and around their home, beauty was everywhere. When I married, they selected a wedding gift from among their favorite pieces, an elegant Italian candy dish that still sits on my piano.

But as my teacher aged, he seemed to sense he was not likely to live much longer. The brightness was gone from his eyes, his iris blossoms no longer seemed so important to him, and his magnificent Steinway Grand, from which once poured beautiful music, sat silent. This was the period in which he pondered the life choices he had made and shared with me his questions about their ultimate value. A sad wistfulness seemed to have filled his heart. That's what he wanted to talk about. I just listened, but as he shared his deepest doubts, I thought I was hearing echoes of *Ecclesiastes*.

Years later after I had moved to Silicon Valley, on an early fall afternoon, Stan had invited me to his home. We began conversation over coffee and strawberry blintzes in his sunken living room with wall to wall glass overlooking the garden, and I was struck with the garden's meticulous grooming and the flow of colors in the flowers. Eventually I asked him how much time he spent in creating such detailed beauty. "Eleven hours a week!" An interior decorator educated in New York, he loved beauty and worked hard at creating it, but he could not shake a feeling of emptiness that lingered after his accomplishment of such beauty. That's why he had invited me to his home.

Nothing is wrong with beauty in sight and sound; it enhances life. But it does not ultimately satisfy if it becomes the purpose for living.

Pleasure seeking is as natural as breathing.

The love of pleasure flows out of our natural needs and desires. Most of us tend to "go for it," often to excess. I think of my own enjoyment of a cup of Kona coffee with a breakfast burrito overlooking the ocean at a Maui beachside café. This kind of down time can contribute much to restoring and preserving good health, both mental and physical. Pleasant moments add pleasure to life, but they do not give it meaning. Our task is to figure out the right kind of pleasure— how much is enough and what value we should realistically expect from it.

If you were ever around people who spend time in such exotic places as the Greek Corfu Island or Jamaica's Ocho Rios or the South of France, it would be easy to be lured by the illusion that life is all about pleasure. It's been said, "The rich are always finding ways to let you know they can afford to be somewhere else." However, access to such soothing and sophisticated places is off limits for most people of the world. To spend time in these places takes very deep pockets, lots of personal freedom, and a stable social and political environment. For most of us, it isn't often that all of these conditions come together at one time, and even when they do, it's only for a brief tenuous period of time.

However, all these fortuitous factors did come together for King Solomon, and he seized the moment.

He plunged fully into pleasure seeking as an end in itself. The striking thing about Solomon's quest for pleasure, in contrast to most modern pleasure connoisseurs, is the wide variety of pleasures he pursued, and all in a geographic area about the size of Vermont. As you go through his long list of indulgences, you can probably identify with some of the things you do or would like to do.

Some of his pursuits were elaborations of ordinary experiences.

Solomon found great pleasure in advancing the technology of his time to improve domestic productivity, enhance military security, and secure political hegemony. His advances in husbandry and horticulture helped improve and secure Israel's food supply. His cultural achievements in the performing arts were outstanding. He seemed to find great enjoyment in working hard at serious study and scientific inquiry.

I can easily imagine Solomon spending a day at the California State Fair and checking out ancient breeds of cattle from Africa that ranchers from Colorado and California have brought to American range land to save them from Africa's droughts, famines, and political turmoil. I can see him amusing himself at the curiosity of the Nubian goats and their willingness to engage with fairgoers. I see him smiling at children checking out the multicolored chickens that have grown so tame that they allow children to stroke their soft feathers. But this king would go far beyond such simple pleasures as a day at the Fair.

Pleasures built on universal human needs were indulged to the extreme, food and drink being two of the most obvious. We die quickly if deprived of the necessities of food and water, but Solomon was constantly coming up with endless refinements on food. So many, in fact, that when the visiting Queen of Sheba saw his riches and the banquet table of food set before her, with solid gold drinking cups, she exclaimed, *"The report I heard in my own country about your achievements and your wisdom is true. But I did not believe these things until I came and saw with my own eyes. Indeed, not even half was told me; in wisdom and wealth you have far exceeded the report I heard"* (1Kings 10:6, 7). Solomon far outdid current state dinners at Buckingham Palace or the White House.

Try to imagine where the author of *Ecclesiastes* might go today for the finest in food and drink if he lived near you? If he lived close to me in the Sacramento area, I believe he would go straight to Napa Valley and St. Helena, only a couple of hours away. His first stop would be at the famous Mondavi Winery to taste a Merlot and admire sculptures of Italian-born Beniamino Bufano. Next he would go to Beringer Winery to choose a Chardonnay for the squab dinner planned for his invited delegation of foreign business leaders. As part of their introduction to California, he would arrange a visit to the world-famous culinary academy at St. Helena. Before they returned to their homelands, he would plan a final lunch on the balcony of *L'auberg du Soleil.* That experience alone would cement their desire to do business with their extraordinary host.

These distinguished guests might even return on their own with their spouses to satisfy the desire to linger in Napa Valley and enjoy an unforgettable lunch on the Napa Wine Train, all while marveling at the stunning scenery from Napa to St. Helena and back. If it's a spring day, their view would be filled with blossoms of lavender and white wisteria covering the walls of old wineries. In the gentle days of early fall, they would see the classic harvests of Napa Valley's incomparable vineyards.

If the author of *Ecclesiastes* had lived in Paris, he would surely have spent a long vacation in the Burgundy region to taste wines crafted by famous vintners from the grapes of that region's valleys and hillsides. He would definitely have needed a designated driver for this excursion, no matter what his claims might be about moderation.

I have been fortunate to work or travel in several countries. Those experiences have given me time to find new foods and new dishes that have left in me a desire to enjoy exquisite tastes once again. Things like fresh calamansi juice in the Philippines, curried goat and Champagne Cola (non-alcoholic) in Jamaica, lamb cutlets and warm shraak bread at *Haret Jdoundna*, an enchanting garden restaurant in Madaba, Jordan, or a sopsky salad in Prague, Czech Republic, and a perfect wiener schnitzel in the Austrian Vienna Woods at a historic restaurant across the road from the trout stream and path where Beethoven walked and got his inspiration for the Ninth Symphony, the familiar *Ode to Joy*. My recommendation is, if you travel, explore local food. It's a great adventure, though a great challenge to keep one's appetite under control.

Apart from enjoying new and unusual food, most of us have palates that still tug at us for the food of our childhood, such as a grandmother's apple pie, a mother's potato salad, pot roast, and angel food cake, and a favorite holiday candy or cookie. That is especially true of immigrants. When moving to a new country and an unfamiliar culture, the last adjustment immigrants make is to fully embrace the food of their new country. That's normal.

Some people, of course, take their enjoyment of food to the extreme. I knew one couple who took many "recreational food vacations," a nice phrase for overeating. After each trip they could spend a whole afternoon describing the meals they had, then the long walks they took to become hungry enough to take on the next meal. Steering clear of Overeaters Anonymous, they were not in good health. Their doctor finally gave up on them. Like Solomon, they had the time and the means to indulge.

Solomon demanded the best settings to serve his international cuisine.

That meant, not merely gorgeous table settings, but beautiful palaces as well. If he had lived in Southern California and planned to build in Hollywood, he would have checked his file of unlisted numbers to call the late Frank Lloyd Wright or Frank Gehry, who designed Facebook's new headquarters in Silicon Valley. Solomon might well have incorporated some of the revolutionary architectural ideas of controversial Le Corbusier.

Copies of *Architectural Digest, Sunset, Better Homes and Gardens* and closely consulted books on elaborate structures usually found only in libraries or in the offices of professional architects would be regular reading for Solomon. All structures commissioned by him would have to be structurally sound, earthquake resistant, and appealing to the eye, right down to the smallest details. Furnishings for different houses would likely have been selected from Italian Modern, French Country, Scandinavian Minimalist, Moroccan or Chinese Traditional.

Solomon demanded grand gardens to compliment his grand houses.

Solomon might have gone to Vancouver Island, Canada, to tour the Butchart Gardens. He would have studied first-hand the flora and examined the ingenuity it took to turn that old limestone quarry into a world famous sunken garden. To study plants easily grown in Jerusalem, he would have taken his botanists to visit the Ba'hai Gardens in Haifa. His demands for well-designed diversity would've led him to study English gardens with their multicolored border plantings, French and Italian formal gardens with their perfect symmetry, and Japanese gardens with their astonishing simplicity and tranquility.

Solomon put great importance on his herds.

Perhaps Solomon's interest in his herds was not only for wealth, but also for their beauty as an ornament to his vast properties. An affluent American family on the Mid-Atlantic coast kept a small herd of Black Angus cattle just to admire their beauty as they grazed on a pasture of deep green grass that sloped down to a sandy beach and the blue ocean beyond. Who would not enjoy a scene like that?

But Solomon would have also bred cattle for their meat and for their role in resisting eye diseases caused by the bright Middle Eastern sun. Solomon had vast scientific knowledge, so he would have known what my late father-in-law knew, who was a veterinarian with a big animal practice in Colorado. He said that ranchers on the high plains, where there was a lot of sunlight, often preferred Black Angus because they seemed to have less eye cancer than white-faced cattle. Also, he said, they were better scroungers for sparse grass in areas with limited rainfall. As for food, I'm sure both Solomon and my father-in-law could say, "I can look at the backend of a steer and tell you how much marble fat will be in the steaks."

With his wealth, Solomon might well have underwritten stock shows, not unlike the annual Denver Stock Show. So many different kinds of livestock and the diversity of breeds made for a fascinating day. The first whiff of the odor we got at the opening gate of those stock shows was our signal that a great day was just ahead.

Solomon obviously loved to eat. That's one reason why he always bred the best herds of sheep and goats, which have always been staples in the Middle East for meat, hides, wool, and dairy products.

Advanced technologies were critical for national development.

Solomon pioneered production of metals, construction of reservoirs for desert irrigation, and development of new weapons for military strength. These accomplishments enabled Solomon to achieve and maintain national superiority in the Middle East.

In this century Solomon would keep up on weekly sports.

Solomon's daily "to do" list would include at least a glance at the latest sports news. Did the San Jose Sharks ice hockey team overpower the Chicago Black

Hawks last night? What's happening in the NBA and the NFL? What players will be traded? International soccer surely would have been on his radar screen.

When my son was in high school in Vienna, Austria he played goalie on his soccer team, and I took him to a game between the national teams of Austria and Hungary. Talk about a charged atmosphere! We sat behind Hungarian fans, whose communist government did allow its "politically reliable" citizens an evening in the free world to shout out support for their home team. When goals were made, they sang, they swayed, and they passed the cognac back and forth as everyone took a swig, immersed in the pleasure of the moment.

Years later, when the World Cup was held in the U.S., the Brazilian team rapidly won over so many fans that when the final game was played, I felt compelled to duck out of a convention in Orlando, Florida to find a television where I could watch them win the Cup. Solomon certainly would not have missed it either, nor a World Series nor a Super Bowl.

Degrading indulgences gradually became part of the mix.

By the time Solomon approached the end of his life, had it been available, he probably would have downloaded the Rolling Stones' cultural classic, *(I Can't Get No) Satisfaction.* The diminishing returns from pleasure hollowed out his life, weakened his family, and wrecked the morality of his nation. His tragic legacy was a divided nation, irrevocably split into Northern and Southern Kingdoms. Pagan worship became widespread, and the One True God was widely abandoned. Such were the sad results of his life-long indulgences.

Exploring the categories of Solomon's incessant pleasure seeking can help us become wise in establishing self-imposed limits on our own impulses and inclinations. Some of Solomon's pleasures are abhorred today by those of us who believe in a full range of human rights for all individuals. His unchecked desires, grandiose achievements, and extreme indulgences came at tremendous cost to many of his own subjects and to outsiders caught in his web of adventures. Over time, he chose to do exactly what God had specifically commanded rulers not to do. *"The king, moreover, must not acquire great numbers of horses for himself or make his people return to Egypt to get more of them, for the Lord has told you, 'You are not to go back that way again.' He must not take many wives, or his heart will be led astray. He must not accumulate large amounts of silver and gold"* (Deuteronomy 17:16, 17).

For Solomon, money was as important as women.

Solomon amassed and hoarded tons of gold and silver that he received as gifts from other nations and from high taxation of his own people. This stockpiled wealth bred resentment in the population, so much so that when his son, Rehoboam, took the throne after Solomon's death, an uprising in the northern provinces forced him out. A former servant of Solomon, Jeroboam, became the ruler of the ten northern tribes. Rehoboam was left with only the southern tribe of Judah, which included Jerusalem, and the tribe of Benjamin.

By the time Solomon was old and dissipated, he reached the conclusion that pleasure and wealth were not all they were cracked up to be.

What happened to Solomon's prayer life during his 40-year reign?

I wonder if Solomon prayed at all after he became rich and powerful and filled with pride. When he first became king, he humbly asked God for the noblest blessings. *"Now, O Lord my God, you have made your servant king in place of my father David. But I am only a little child and do not know how to carry out my duties. Your servant is here among the people you have chosen, a great people, too numerous to count or number. So give your servant a discerning heart to govern your people and to distinguish between right and wrong" (1 Kings 3:7-9).* God replied, *"Since you have asked for this and not for long life or wealth for yourself, nor have you asked for the death of your enemies but for discernment in administering justice, I will do what you have asked. I will give you a wise and discerning heart, so that there will never have been anyone like you, nor will there ever be" (1 Kings 3:11, 12).*

So what happened to his prayer life between the ages of 25 and 55? We can never know for sure, but we do know he gave in to his natural desires without regard for the guidelines God has given to keep our behaviors under control. God did create us with free will, free to choose, but also, to live with the consequences of our choices, good or bad. We all have choices about pleasure. Just be wise enough to hit the brakes if your heavy foot is stuck on the indulgence accelerator.

Solomon's over indulgence left him wanting as a human being and left his brilliantly built empire ready to crumble. And it all happened quickly, over a period of 40 years.

The following scripture explains what went wrong in Solomon's life. *"King Solomon, however loved many foreign women besides Pharaoh's daughter – Moabites, Ammonites, Edomites, Sidonians and Hittites. They were from nations about which the Lord had told the Israelites, 'You must not intermarry with them, because they will surely turn your hearts after theirs gods.' Nevertheless, Solomon held fast to them in love. As Solomon grew old, his wives turned his heart after other gods, and his heart was not fully devoted to the Lord his God, as the heart of David his father had been"*
(1 Kings 11:1-4).

Reflections:

1 - As you age what safeguards do you have in place to avoid Solomon's mistakes?

2 - Are there areas of your life that are especially susceptible to overindulgence? What have been and what are the consequences? Any plans to deal with this?

3 - In what ways have your parents and grandparents demonstrated areas of restraint and areas of indulgences in pleasure in their lives? How have their behavior patterns influenced your behaviors?

CHAPTER 6
HELP THE OPPRESSED
AND UNFORTUNATE

"If you see the poor oppressed in a district, and justice and rights denied, do not be surprised at such things; for one official is eyed by a higher one, and over them both are others higher still." *(Ecclesiastes 5:8).*

People who do not have the values, beliefs, or culture for empathy expressed in these statements of King Solomon may evaluate the poor as less than human and treat them as men with evil in their hearts did when these scriptures were written 3,000 years ago.

In contrast to oppression, *"When justice is done, it brings joy to the righteous but terror to evildoers"* *(Proverbs 21:15)*. God's law was embedded in King Solomon's conscience in spite of his selfish indulgences and unjust treatment of his own countrymen. He could not free himself from the fact that human beings are not to be oppressed, enslaved, or denied their rights. It is unsettling to be in the presence of oppression. Those most vulnerable are people in absolute poverty, without adequate food, shelter or clothing. The hungry and the homeless are too cold on winter nights or too hot in summer heat, unprotected from all extremes of weather. The vulnerable are helpless children, war-ravaged refugees, and people fleeing from religious oppression or trapped in political persecution, all of them targets of irrational hatred.

Oppression is common.

In the late 1940's, the onset of Communist control and oppression in Czechoslovakia was especially destructive to the human spirit. It was not possible to express anything close to being fully human under the regime's constant surveillance and severe punishment for any deviance from communist ideology.

After 40 years of this oppression, life could only become whole again if freedom came. In 2002, the city of Prague and the Confederation of Political Prisoners built a memorial with the haunting title, Disappearing Man, which gives a sequential portrayal of man in progressive decay. The memorial consists of seven bronze figures ascending a flight of stairs. On the lowest step the man is whole and going up the stairs. But each of the next sculptures loses limbs, and their bodies are breaking open. At the last statue, only a sliver of a man is left. Finally, there is no man. This stunning sequence is a symbolic representation of the terrible fate experienced by political prisoners under communism. More than 200,000 were arrested, over 150,000 forced into exile, approximately 4,500 died in prison, and over 500 others were either executed or shot trying to escape. The plaque on the sculptures reads: "This memorial to the victims of communism is dedicated to all victims, not only those who were jailed or executed, but also those whose lives were ruined by totalitarian despotism." Only when men and women are truly free can they be fully human.

The destructive force of ethnic hatred fosters vicious and gross oppression.

I remember a quiet spring morning in Auschwitz, one of Europe's most visited Nazi death camps. Just as the sun broke through a gray sky and birds began to sing, the Polish guide directed our attention to the firing squad wall. In that terrible moment, I could imagine hearing gunshots and seeing innocent people fall to the ground, drowning out the music of birds and darkening the beauty of the morning sun. The scene in my mind was so real that I don't recall anything else the guide was saying. Some people I've met in Europe who survived the horrors of the death camps found ways to deal constructively with that awful part of their past. They rebuilt their lives. Others did not. Auschwitz represents, perhaps, the ultimate oppression, but in later years there has been the mass horrors of Cambodia, Rwanda, and Sudan — plus many other similar tragedies that have gone unpublicized and unknown to a world of people too busy and too preoccupied with their own daily concerns to take notice.

The Nazis liquidated so many doctors, teachers, professors, community leaders, pastors, and priests that they destroyed much of the brain trust and social capital of Europe. This may have contributed to their loss of WWII. When I visited the Lublin/Majdanek death camp in eastern Poland, I took time to read the long lists of names, meticulously preserved and organized by nationality, ethnic identity, and sexual orientation. Citizens of at least 50 countries died there. Many of these people clearly would have been among the most capable contributors to European society and to the German war machine. What stunned and sickened me most at this camp were the ovens, completely intact, not partially destroyed as at Auschwitz. The Russian army overran eastern Poland so quickly that the Nazis had no time to dismantle the evidence of their atrocities. My Polish friend said these ovens were built to consume nearly a thousand bodies every 24 hours. Just before the bodies were taken to the ovens, they were placed on a concrete slab where all the gold was removed from their teeth and anything else of value that may have been swallowed.

As we silently left the building on that beautiful, golden Polish autumn day, I was too emotionally drained to make any comment. The hideous visual reality of what had happened there left me both speechless and physically nauseated. How thankful I was that I had not eaten lunch. Only then did I understand why my host's wife had somberly said as we approached the crematorium, "I'll stay in the car."

In varying degrees, oppression and persecution exist today on every continent for irrational reasons of race, tribe, class, ethnicity, political opinions, religious convictions, economic standing, and educational status. Some places, obviously, are worse than others, but oppression can erupt like a volcano anywhere. When it does, it becomes the responsibility of true human beings to refuse to put on blinders or seek distractions to erase what you see. A good life cannot be at peace in the presence of injustice.

The Nazi in all of us.

"Could this happen again?" That was the question asked on a trip I led through Central Europe as our bus headed north from Auschwitz. In response, one of the travelers, a woman who worked at Stanford University, brought up the 1971 situation where normal college students could oppress fellow students. In the Stanford experiment students were separated into prisoners in degrading uniforms stamped with impersonal identity numbers or guards in authoritative military style uniforms. The setting simulated a 24/7 prison. Within 36 hours, the first "prisoner" suffered an emotional breakdown. Others soon followed. The "guards" had begun to behave in abusive ways toward the "prisoners." The planned two-week experiment had to be called off in six days!

Another experiment in this kind of behavior is the 1961 Milgram Obedience/Authority experiment at Yale University. The results of this experiment prove that "good people" will inflict great pain on fellow human beings under the right set of circumstances.

This may explain in part the horrors of German death camps and the Soviet Gulag. Also, greed, grandiosity, twisted political philosophy, radical religious beliefs, sectarian hatred, and even physical conditions that trap people in a survival mode of dog-eat-dog, every-man-for-himself existence may lead to ruthless actions toward others.

So as we rode on to Warsaw, reality set in: "Yes, Auschwitz could happen again!" But even in that situation, filled with the worst possible treatment of others, Oskar Schindler, an empathetic factory owner and risk taker, saved as many prisoners as possible. Our tour group also visited the Schindler Museum, close to Auschwitz. We walked through the gate into the factory grounds and climbed the steps to Schindler's simple office. We saw the plain desk where he faced his helplessness in saving more people. I had to ponder what I might have done in that same situation had I sat there. And what about the others who were traveling with me? What might they have chosen to do? In deciding to carry out his mission, Schindler must have been a person of great inner strength to accept the risk, *"If I perish, I perish."* After the war, he also had to carry forever the burden of victims he loved and longed to save, but couldn't. The images of the desperation in their eyes would always be memories that would haunt him.

In a different **WWII** setting, a German officer saved the life of "The Pianist."

This German officer was captured by the Russians when they took Warsaw. The Pianist, out of gratitude for the compassion of the German officer who saved him, desperately tried to find that officer in the Soviet prison camps, but to no avail. Today, the families of the Pianist and the German officer have not forgotten each other. Friends in Warsaw tell me that their children remain in touch. When I asked those friends how they evaluated the movie, *The Pianist,* they said it was one of the most accurate interpretations of the World War II era and how people treated each other. "There were good Poles and bad Poles," they said, "good Germans and bad Germans, good Jews and bad Jews." Indeed, one of the most famous survivors of the holocaust, the late Elie Wiesel, has said of the great caring and compassion that accompanied all the cruelty and callousness of the death camps, "The mystery of good is just as unexplainable as the mystery of evil."

After all my endless days of traveling and my endless hours of talking with people who observed or experienced the oppression of the Nazi and Soviet regimes, I have come to several conclusions. First, I firmly believe that empathy, compassion, and forgiveness, along with an unflinching commitment to high moral standards, are the most effective deterrents to discarding our moral beliefs and betraying our moral obligations. Second, I equally believe that once those moral standards are removed there are no barriers left to oppressing and persecuting others with total abandon. The potential for evil and for nobility exists in all of us.

The movies, *Schindler's List* and *The Pianist* portray the 20th Century in its awful messiness, but Oskar Schindler and the German officer did what was right for a good life, even in the worst circumstances. These are worthy examples for all of us to follow.

Reach out to tragic victims of human trafficking.

Sex trafficking and slave labor are among today's worst international problems. Two well-documented cases of the raw nature of these kinds of oppression involve the U.S., Russia, and Mexico. Thankfully, these stories end well due to daring rescues by honest and alert government authorities.

A nineteen-year-old girl with the pseudonym of Olga ended up alone and frightened in Moscow, making her the perfect target for Russian sex traffickers. Both her father and boyfriend had been murdered by a Russian mob, leaving her desperate to get out of Moscow. A new "friend" introduced her to Alexander Rashkovsky, a man who claimed to be looking for girls to work at good jobs in America. He offered her a new life with transportation to the United States and a position as an "assistant" once she got there. She gratefully accepted his offer, believing she would be safe and secure in America, where rights are upheld and enforced. Besides, she thought, anywhere is better than Moscow. His pitch to her is the typical tactic of slave traders. Soon the trap door slams shut on the bait, a brutal reality sets in, and such girls realize they are trapped and feel helpless. After Rashkovsky purchased the tickets, Olga says, he made it clear there was no backing out of the agreement, telling them, "If anybody tries to run away, I'm not going to deal with you, I'm just going to cut your head off."

Olga boarded the plane with four other girls. At that moment, they became the property of the international slave trader. Olga's plane was headed to Mexico where Rashkovsky intended to smuggle them across the U.S. border. But as they began the border crossing at customs, the quick-thinking Olga made her surprise move by speaking in the Russian language. An alert border checkpoint guard investigated the situation and rescued the women. Rashkovsky was convicted and died in a California prison. Olga was given a visa for human trafficking victims and stayed in the U.S.

In Hidalgo, Mexico, a "coyote" told Antonio that he could be smuggled across the border for work in California. While in route, the coyote's group of forty people became separated. Antonio was taken to a smuggler in Arizona where he was held until he could pay the smuggling fee. Unable to pay, he was told that he would be sent to a tomato field where he would be paid $150 a day. A driver, El Chucal, took him and seventeen others on a three-day bus trip to a Southern Florida work camp. Not once on the trip were they were al-lowed to leave the bus, not even for restroom breaks.

Once in Florida, Antonio heard El Chucal negotiating with Abel Cuello, the owner of the camp, for his price. That's when he realized he was a slave, sold just like an animal, and locked in a room with several others. When Cuello took them to the tomato field, they were controlled with threats and grisly stories of runaways being murdered. After four months of backbreaking labor, Antonio made a successful escape while Cuello slept. Antonio obtained a visa, and he now works in agriculture for legal pay.[1]

Justice and mercy are twin threads interwoven throughout the Bible.

Biblical justice resists all forms of favoritism. Moses wrote, *"Always judge your neighbors fairly, neither favoring the poor nor showing deference to the rich"* (*Leviticus 19:15*). Generations later the Prophet, Zechariah reminded the people, *"Judge fairly and honestly, and show mercy and kindness to one another. Do not oppress widows, orphans, foreigners, and poor people. And do not make evil plans to harm each other"* (*Zechariah 7:9-10*).

Justice requires laws that are carefully crafted to ensure freedom and protection for all citizens. It further requires leaders to submit to and enforce those laws. However, if laws are unjust, we need to respond with discernment, consultation with others, and act in a productive, helpful, and positive way to change those laws to be just and fair. No one, including a government's highest leaders, is above the law. This was a founding principle of the nation of ancient Israel. If practiced, this noble principle negates both corruption and oppression.

At a personal level, if we develop sensitivity and compassion for individuals and groups suffering under oppression, our own lives will be richer and more satisfying. A good life is not possible when experiencing oppression, ignoring it, or perpetrating it.

Reflections:

1 - How have you, either as an individual or as a group you belong to, helped an oppressed person or group?

2 - How would you develop a philosophy of life or a set of spiritual beliefs that would help you avoid such mistakes as in the Stanford or Yale experiments and in real life?

3 - What practical steps are you taking or teaching to help others recover from religious, political, sexual, or financial oppression?

CHAPTER 7
"DETAIL" YOUR LIFE
ALONG WITH YOUR CAR

"As dead flies give perfume a bad smell, so a little folly out-weighs wisdom and honor" (Ecclesiastes 10:1).

Detailing your life is like
detailing your car.

Even a cheap car wash will make your car look better, but it's polishing the wheels, dressing the tires, and cleaning the carpet and upholstery that show off a car at its best. Detailing a car on a regular basis insures better resale value. Also, meticulous care of each part of the car often uncovers needed repairs. While detailing a classic Corvette, two fellows discovered that the car's body was about to come loose from the frame. That discovery paid off handsomely. What happened with that Corvette can also happen with your life.

We've focused on some basic building blocks of a good life, such as enjoying work, family, friendships, food, and clothing. We've looked at character traits, attitudes, and behaviors that round out a good life. Detailing one's life also includes what to do and what not to do in specific situations, when to take action and when to refrain. *Proverbs,* like *Ecclesiastes,* has many guidelines on detailing one's life. The warning that an *"ounce of foolishness can outweigh a pound of wisdom and honor"* hammers home the danger of recklessly ignoring details. Here are some important areas for detailing your life.

Keep your cool and be wise in handling criticisms.

"If a ruler's anger rises against you, do not leave your post; calmness can lay great errors to rest" (Ecclesiastes 10:4), and *"Do not revile the king even in your thoughts, or curse the rich in your bedroom, because a bird on the wing may report what you say"* (Ecclesiastes 10:20).

Applied to your employment, if the boss is angry because you made a mistake, exhibit a calm, quiet spirit. Hunker down until his storm of emotion passes. His or her anger, though temporarily directed at you, may actually be linked to problems in his or her own personal relationships. Some people in positions of authority use explosions of anger as a management tool, yelling things like, "I'm only trying to help you!" It was said of shoe-pounding Soviet Premier Nikita Khrushchev that the canny leader never made the mistake of *losing* his temper, he merely *used* his temper. Other bosses, perhaps threatened by your talents, may deliberately undermine your standing with both fellow employees and higher ups, eliminating the possibility of a promotion or raise in salary.

Whether a boss's angry actions toward you are justified or not, defending yourself at that emotion-filled moment almost always makes matters worse. Sponge up the outburst. Avoid the same mistake again, if that's the issue. If not, and if no opportunity presents itself to get on good terms with your boss, it may be time to quietly begin the search for a different job or position and a new boss. If so, try to leave at such a time and in such a way as not to burn any bridges.

A boss's anger may serve a positive purpose. It reveals something is wrong: perhaps with what someone is doing, what you might be doing, or how you or someone may be interpreting and responding to the situation. Rather than allowing anger to control you, let it be a guide. *"A hot-tempered man stirs up dissension, but a patient man calms a quarrel" (Proverbs 15:18)*. This scripture offers wise advice for keeping your anger under careful control. Neil Clark Warren, author of *Make Anger Your Ally*, gives practical steps on how to get positive results when you experience anger, such as figuring out and declaring what you wanted, but didn't get, that generated your anger. His suggestions always work for me if I implement them. Above all, never deny the presence of anger.

One of the most blatant examples I have witnessed of an uncontrolled outburst of denied anger was in a board meeting with thirteen men. In front of everyone, one man yelled insultingly at another man with whom he disagreed, and then ended his outburst with the ridiculous disclaimer, "I'm not angry!" It was a flat denial of an emotion that flew in the face of his conduct. To cap this little farce, he then stood up and stormed out of the room. It was clear to all the rest of us that this man was angry to the point of fury, but he seemed totally unaware of the intensity and the impact of his own emotions. That was the last evening he was a part of that group.

You've probably "been there, seen that." Maybe even, "been there, done that." *Proverbs* says, *"A man's wisdom gives him patience; it is to his glory to overlook an offense" (Proverbs 19:11)*. Leaders, especially, in all types of positions, should exercise great caution in guarding their speech when they are frustrated. A position of authority does not give license to yell, make misguided statements, or verbally abuse someone. Moses, the great leader of the ancient Israelites, became frustrated with his irritating followers, lost his cool, and spoke in anger, *"By the waters of Meribah... trouble came to Moses because of them... and rash words came from his lips" (Psalm 106:32, 33)*. Generations later, his outburst is still recalled and used as a warning for everyone against letting misplaced anger motivate actions.

Hold back on criticizing others.

Ecclesiastes offers a "caution light" on criticisms, saying: *"Never make light of the king even in your thoughts."* This warning, if heeded, would put some Talk Radio out of business and silence much of what passes today as political discourse. The faults and failures of people in highly visible and powerful positions make them natural targets for constant criticism, but it's wise to refrain. Comments at work about a boss or colleague that even hint of criticism can easily be embellished by someone else. A few carefully crafted or careless synonyms can turn your mild well-meaning comments into sounding like full-blown, hostile criticism, with damaging repercussions. Criticism might also take the silent form of passive-aggressive behavior, like sulking, evading, stonewalling, smirking, or rolling one's eyes.

Especially dangerous are critical comments or witty sarcasms released on social media. They spread faster than one of California's wind-fueled wild fires. Anything in print, anywhere, should be approached with thoughtful self-censorship. That includes personal letters. Apply this test: "Is it OK if this shows up on the front page of the *New York Times?*"

When traveling in foreign countries, beware of making any comments that are less than complimentary about the host country, especially to hotel employees and taxi drivers. Some taxi drivers in major cities may be government informers. Use caution in talking with a traveling companion in your native language while in a cab or public place where you can be overheard. Drivers and bystanders may understand more of your language than you think.

Avoid some subjects altogether. When traveling in Iron Curtain countries before communist governments collapsed, I avoided all discussions of anything political. If nationals made derogatory comments about their government, I listened blank-faced. I never knew to whom I might be speaking. He could easily have been a government informer in disguise. In some cases, I was sure that's exactly what he was. Staying on neutral subjects such as your appreciation and enjoyment of the food, architecture, arts, opera, and sports, especially soccer, were usually safe subjects. Watch out not to bite on the bait of open-ended questions.

When South Africa was in the midst of the struggle to end apartheid, a California activist arrived on the scene with her agenda to show the nationals how to solve their problem. She was pulled aside by a responsible national leader, who agreed that apartheid should end, but advised, "Remember, the Lord of the *ends* is also the Lord of the *means*." To arrive in South Africa with her presumptuous agenda was criticism in itself. Fortunately, she listened and behaved appropriately. The payoff was that her more modest presence likely encouraged nationals in their long-term efforts to end that injustice. So no matter how bad things seem, uncontrolled anger and harsh criticisms are land mines. Stay clear.

Nail down life's risk factors.

"Whoever digs a pit may fall into it; whoever breaks through a wall may be bitten by a snake. Whoever quarries stones may be injured by them; whoever splits logs may be endangered by them" (Ecclesiastes. 10:8, 9).

Such are the risks of life. In other words, identify and stay alert for all possible risks. Risk management is serious business.

The monumental Gateway Arch in St. Louis, Missouri, designed by Finnish-American architect Eero Saarein, is phenomenal. It is stunningly beautiful and strikingly simple in both lines and texture. Whether viewed close up from the ground or seen looking down from the air, it is magnificent. This is especially true in brilliant sunlight against a backdrop of approaching thunder clouds or when bathed in the changing hues of a colorful sunset. The dizzying view from inside the Arch looking down on Busch Stadium is not for those afraid of heights.

Just as amazing as the Arch's beauty is that not one person is reported to have lost his life during its construction. Prior to construction, safety experts took great pains to identify and to address every possible risk. Specific work policies and training methods were designed to minimize and eliminate any threat to worker safety. When it comes to dealing with risks, the "engineering management ethics" of that leadership team is worthy of serious study. They got it right.

Risks have to be lived with, no way around it. Fed up with his mother's unrelenting harping to always, "be careful," my uncle one day responded, "Mother, it's dangerous to be alive!" His comment did nothing to ease her fears, but being careful could be one reason she lived to be 95. If there was a risk anywhere, she found it. However, people who are afraid and unwilling to take some risks may achieve little in life. Even worse, they may miss out on much of life's greatest enjoyment in overcoming dangers and conquering difficulties to reach worthy goals.

In dealing with national security, military analysts and policy specialists responsible for managing relations with other nations ask a basic question in evaluating complex and dangerous situations: "What is the worst possible outcome in this situation?" They craft policies to address those possibilities and then move on to deal with lesser risks. When the U.S. Department of State is deciding where to put diplomatic outposts, "risk to personnel and value of presence" are both weighed seriously. The goal is to minimize risk, but reap benefits. This approach to risk works in all areas of life.

Individuals undergoing surgery or major dental work sign off on a "risk list" that often includes potential stroke, heart attack, paralysis, and infections. Surgical teams know these risks exist. They are legally bound to advise their patients of such negative possibilities. And they have response systems in place should any potential risk become a real and present danger.

Some risks in life are too great to take. Some must be lived with. Some are necessary for survival. But identifying them always puts you ahead of the game.

Aim for excellence, not perfection.

"Do not be overrighteous, neither be overwise - why destroy yourself? Do not be overwicked, and do not be a fool - why die before your time? It is good to grasp the one and not let go of the other. The man who fears God will avoid all extremes" *(Ecclesiastes 7:16-18).*

An observation about human behavior in a letter addressed to the first Christians in Rome says, *"All have sinned and fall short of the glory of God"* *(Romans 3:23).* No matter how intense the effort, no matter how lofty the intent, perfection won't happen for anyone in any endeavor. Insisting on perfection can drive perfectionists and everyone around them nuts. A more realistic goal, one equally noble, is excellence. *Philippians,* a short document authored by the Apostle Paul, is often identified as the Christian Mental Health Charter of the *New Testament.* Its focus is on excellence, not perfection. Paul said of himself, *"I do not consider myself to have yet taken hold of it (the righteousness of God). But one thing I do: Forgetting what is behind and straining toward what is ahead, I press on toward the goal (Philippians 3:13, 14).* Later in *Philippians,* he called on his readers to *"think about things that are excellent"* *(Philippians 4:8).*

Perfection backfires. It often deteriorates into rigid legalism, leading to judgmental attitudes toward others and self-condemnation for oneself for failure to meet such an impossible standard. Ironically, perfectionists are seldom high producers of anything. Olympic athletes such as Michael Phelps or music virtuosos such as Itzhak Pearlman know they will not perform perfectly, but they aim always to do their very best. And they're great.

While doing volunteer work with the San Francisco Symphony, a speaker told us that when recordings are prepared for radio broadcasts, all performances in a week of concerts are carefully compared. One movement from a Beethoven symphony might be chosen from the Thursday performance, another two movements from the Saturday performance, and another from Sunday. The fact is, performances of the same composition in different concerts in the same week by the same musicians and the same conductor vary in quality. No performance is "perfect." All are good, and some are just slightly better than others.

In terms of our efforts to be just, moral, and responsible in our personal behavior, we often fail in spite of the best intentions. Failure is a good word to keep activated in our vocabulary. By relaxing a bit and aiming for consistent excellence in contrast to insane perfection, we are more likely to become the persons we believe we should be, achieve what we desire, and be able to get along with others in the process.

The late esteemed philosopher Sir Karl Popper was once a visiting professor at the University of Denver. In his class, he was asked, "When do you quit rewriting a book and know that it's finished?" He paused, then summed up his view on writing, "I never finish a book; I just abandon it at some point!" That's how realists think and act in their pursuit of excellence.

Elect good leaders.

After communism collapsed in Central/Eastern Europe in 1989, Czechoslovakians elected dissident playwright Vaclav Havel for their president. Many in America viewed him as the Thomas Jefferson of Central Europe because Havel seriously studied our Declaration of Independence. He saw the ideals of freedom, liberty, and justice as universal longings. He committed himself to creating a democratic form of government as a means of securing those rights. He firmly believed those rights have their true origin in our basic humanity, above the authority of any state.

Under communist rule, Havel was one of the key architects of *Charter 77*, a civic initiative that called for implementing rights that were guaranteed in the Czechoslovakian Constitution and in treaties signed by the government. He and the others who signed the *Charter 77* document were officially branded as traitors and renegades. The communist rulers destroyed the original document. They imposed harsh censorship and made many arrests. Havel spent four years in prison, sometimes in solitary confinement. And he was often very ill.

Before this clampdown, hope had flourished in the mid-1960s that the Prague Spring, with a call for a more human face on communism, would bring an end to ruthless oppression. Instead, the Soviets joined forces with hard line Czechs and unleashed a blizzard of renewed suppression. Despite the terrible risks,

Havel refused to give up the quest for freedom for his homeland. He and other dissidents met clandestinely, sometimes over coffee at the Slavia Café near the Vltava River. Ironically, from that café sidewalk is a view of the Grand Castle where one day Havel would have his presidential office. In those difficult days, they kept hope alive, and they pressed on to end the tyranny. Havel inspired others by taking drastic measures to call attention to his country's dire circumstances and to his nation's desperate need for freedom.

Today, that café is still a good place to have an espresso and ponder the insights in Havel's book, *Living in Truth*. He grasped how communism made liars of everyone, "knowing exactly what you'd been told you should say you believe, but really not believing a word of it." As pretense for survival, everyone mastered living a lie. And even after communism was gone, that kind of lying proved to be a habit hard to shake. It is no easy matter to be an authentic human being.

The communist history is not overlooked, but remembered. At the base of the statue of King Charles on Wenceslas Square is a memorial to a young Czech who immolated himself in those dark days as a martyr for freedom's cause. For years, each time I walked past, fresh flowers always adorned that sacred site.

During the short interval between World War I and World War II, Czechoslovakians had experienced freedom and enjoyed a democratic government. They longed to make that memory become real again.

Communism could not crush that longing. It finally emerged in full force in the fall of 1989 in what was called the "Velvet Revolution." It was a transformation that began with a non-violent protest of wall to wall people in historic Wenceslas Square, determined at last to say aloud with their voices what they truly believed in their hearts. Standing with them was a mature, seasoned Vaclav Havel ready to lead the transition from dictatorship to democracy.

The Velvet Revolution unfolded before the world on television.

I had just returned to California from Poland. I had seen what had been happening at border crossings. I was riveted to my TV. My mind raced back 10 years to 1979 when I made my first border crossing into communist Bratislava, Czechoslovakia, less than an hour from Vienna. My American colleague and I met with a young engineer there. As the October sun filtered through lace curtains in the dingy hotel coffee shop, he described how Warsaw Pact troops crushed the Prague Spring. His wife was ready to give birth as this turmoil was going on. He told how afraid he was that on the way to the hospital they might be stopped, forced out of the car, and abandoned on the roadside, with their car arbitrarily confiscated. He said such incidents were not uncommon. He had my full attention, because only an hour earlier at the border our passports were taken, the interior of our van was thoroughly examined, mirrors were rolled under the chassis to check for contraband, and military guards on towers above us watched with machine guns ready to fire if something went awry. This was my first experience without freedom—without freedom of association, freedom of the press, freedom of speech, and freedom of religion.

In another communist country where I taught, you needed a government permit just to own a typewriter. The only works of world philosophers that were available were communist party approved abstracts. I was abruptly told of that fact by a well-educated person at our clandestine meeting when I merely mentioned the names of Kant and Hume. There were so many things one dared not mention. Informers were everywhere.

While I was living in Vienna, an Oxford professor who was meeting clandestinely with university students in Prague to discuss the works of Aristotle was forced out of the country after being there only three weeks. No place was entirely secure for free expression. Everyone was always cautious about what he or she said, how loudly or softly it was said, and what one listened to. I observed that their eyes saw everything, but said nothing.

The first border crossing solidified my commitment to promote human rights and to work for a full range of freedoms for everyone. I can truly say, with Thomas Jefferson, that I have sworn on the altar of God eternal hostility to every form of tyranny over the mind of man. These experiences have instilled in me a constant caution about how careful we must be in choosing those we allow to govern us. Freedom can be easily lost if we carelessly elect the wrong leaders.

Choosing good leaders is part of "detailing" your life.

Without wise governance that protects and preserves the full range of the rights and freedoms guaranteed in the Bill of Rights, it is impossible to control or to shape what we do with our lives. Life degenerates into a series of passive responses, such as the one I often heard in Russia, "Let's wait and see what happens tomorrow." There, it seemed, any new idea, any fresh initiative, any desire to try something new was always met with the response, "It is not possible in our system." If we Americans are to keep the freedoms we so prize, we must always do the heavy lifting of true citizenship, which is to stay fully informed and to make wise choices for our government leaders.

"Woe to you, O land whose king was a servant and whose princes feast in the morning. Blessed are you, O land whose king is of noble birth and whose princes eat at a proper time — for strength and not for drunkenness (Ecclesiastes 10:16, 17).

In monarchies, there may be no choice or chance to replace an inept or evil king short of revolution. However, for the millions who believe in democracies or semi-democratic societies, the electorate bears responsibility for who leads the nation. Are the leaders capable, wise, genuine servants of the people, neither corrupt nor greedy? That buck stops with us, the electorate. An electorate that selects a tyrant bears responsibility for the oppression imposed upon them.

Politics has to do with establishing and managing the ever-shifting relationships among groups and individuals. Therefore, politics matters. Politicians make the laws that control these relationships. If they are lawbreakers or establish laws favorable to some and unfavorable to others, they should be rejected by voters. If the country is managed well by the elected leadership, the electorate deserves credit for wise choices of their leaders.

Good leaders refuse bribes. They refuse to show special favor to the rich or to the poor. They are not partial to one racial or ethnic group over others. They do not presume to think they can live above the law and use their positions as a source of gain. Those principles are as ancient as the Law of Moses.

Politics is an exercise in power relations. Elected officials authorized to use power have a responsibility for personal integrity, for thoughtful legislation, and for fair enforcement. Voters have the responsibility to weed out bad guys by recall, impeachment, or not re-electing them. These matters are vitally important because it takes far more effort to shape a good life in a nation that is governed poorly or recklessly!

As you focus on detailing your life, realize that your life has more parts than your car. It takes great effort to examine those details thoroughly.

Detailing your life is not a
one-time activity.

I advise annual self-reviews. One helpful way to do it is to read the 31 chapters of *Proverbs* in the month of January, one chapter a day. As you read each chapter, ask yourself what it confirms that's in good order in your life, where some slippage has occurred, or where there are flaws that need to be addressed.

For information related to detailing contemporary mundane life management, I like *Bottom Line* for brief, bluntly stated practical helps. As an example, a single page on "Living Longer and Better" covered six important items, among which were suggestions on avoiding gym germs, a few guidelines for taking a nap based on psychological and medical research, and finally how to estimate how much life insurance you need. Truly, wisdom in even the smallest matters is constantly calling out to us in the public square, a description of the gathering place for listeners in King Solomon's days. After you have wrapped up detailing your life with plenty of elbow grease, you just might experience that same wonderful feeling you have when slipping behind the wheel of your freshly detailed car.

Reflections:

1 - What keeps you from reviewing the details of your life? Any plans in place to remove those blocks?

2 - In what settings and with whom do you find it most convenient to review those "details?"

3 - How do you go about helping others identify what "details" may need attention in their lives without alienating them?

CHAPTER 8
KNOW WHAT CAN'T BE CHANGED ABOUT LIFE

"The living know that they will die" (Ecclesiastes 9:5).

Death comes to all.

People who are best adjusted to the reality of death are also among those best adjusted to the reality of life. To avoid or deny the fact of death frustrates efforts to receive the most from life and to give the most to others. It is equally important, however, to acknowledge that death was not supposed to be part of our story. That's why we resist death. The brevity and cessation of life will never feel right because God placed "eternity" in the mind of man. *"He (God) has also set eternity in the hearts of men"* *(Ecclesiastes 3:11).* The longing for continued existence will not go away. Nor should it. It is wise to be urgent, intentional, and persistent about life against the backdrop of death.

Playwrights, poets, musicians and painters all work with the theme of death. J.S. Bach composed four songs about death, the first about untimely death, which opens with a thunderous baritone declaration, "Oh Death, how cruel you are." Untimely death is heavy and hard to deal with. But later in Bach's fourth song, the tone becomes peaceful and engaging as death offers release from suffering and from the limitations of old age. That song opens, "Oh death, what a friend you are." Dealing with death up front is not morbid. To the contrary, it frees us to engage in life more fully. However, no matter how well we conceptually accommodate the reality of death, the loss of someone we love is traumatic. It is emotionally devastating. That's normal. It takes time and effort to establish a new way of life.

Fear of death seems normal for most people. Death encompasses loss of control, inability to know what the experience will actually be like, fear of the unknown, and the uncertainty of how we will die. Will it be sudden or drawn out? Will it include a loss of dignity? Will I experience much pain? Death is a difficult issue. The Apostle Paul, a believer filled with hope, acknowledged the oppressive nature of death when he wrote to believers in Corinth, *The last enemy to be destroyed is death" (1 Corinthians 15:26).*

I believe that Jesus Christ came to rewrite the final story concerning death. The Prophet Isaiah anticipated that day as he prophesied, *"He will destroy the shroud that enfolds all peoples, the sheet that covers all nations; he will swallow up death forever. The Sovereign Lord will wipe away the tears from faces" (Isaiah 25:7, 8).* The final book in the New Testament enriches this promise. *"Then I saw a new heaven and a new earth, for the first heaven and the first earth had passed away and there was no longer any sea. I saw the Holy City, the new Jerusalem, coming down out of heaven from God, prepared as a bride beautifully dressed for her*

husband. And I heard a loud voice from the throne saying, 'Now the dwelling of God is with men, and he will live with them. They will be his people, and God himself will be with them and be their God. He will wipe away every tear from their eyes. There will be no more death or mourning or crying or pain, for the old order of things has passed away"
(Revelation 21:1-4).

This is a very appealing ultimate future, but it is not yet with us. For a good life here and now, other unchangeable factors, also identified as "givens," need to be addressed, especially forging a life of integrity that leads to a good reputation within one's community.

Reputation counts.

"A good name is better than fine perfume" (Ecclesiastes 7:1). Reputation is the public's report card on you or your organization's character. That report is important, because it follows us wherever we go. Your public image can open doors to a better life or it can keep you locked out of many opportunities for success. People do pay attention to reputations.

A college president once commented that one institutional fear he had was a moral failure of faculty or administration. An institution's reputation for integrity might be lost. This is a danger for any organization if the people within it do not act in ways that are consistent with who they claim to be and with the ideals they claim to stand for. If you are part of a group or organization, you share the responsibility to help shape and sustain the group's reputation. If your company offers products or services, you need to help build a reputation for immediate, courteous responses to customer needs and client requests. Some companies develop reputations for shoddy products. Even professionals can be guilty of offering incompetent services. The point is, once a reputation takes root, it tends to stand for a long time. Marketing experts say that even with a full-blown campaign, it takes an average of seven years to change the public's negative perception to a positive perception.

First century church members who did not have good reputations in their wider communities were not considered qualified to hold any of the higher roles of leadership in the church. The Apostle Paul directed his co-worker, Timothy, to instruct Christians in Ephesus, modern Turkey, to select as elders and overseers only those members who were *"above reproach"* *(1 Timothy 3:2)*.

In the era of Facebook, LinkedIn, Twitter, image management is critical for building or destroying reputations. It is imperative to keep in mind how a variety of individuals and groups will respond to what we post. LinkedIn caters to professional groups, like a business lunch. Facebook is like a backyard barbeque for friends and neighbors. Twitter is like a drive through eatery. Think audience. On Facebook, your backyard may include all of North America or Asia. What others think, say and do about our reputations is largely beyond our control, but we are responsible for how we present ourselves. In this regard, we have considerable control over the shaping of our reputations. It's also been said, "You take care of your character and your reputation will take care of itself." We can do much to make ourselves worthy of a good reputation. That reputation still counts is one of life's "givens."

The future cannot be known.

"For who can tell what will happen under the sun" (Ecclesiastes 6:12). Investors try hard to accurately read the economic tea leaves, but they are the first to concede that the future cannot be predicted. Trends can be carefully observed and tracked, but that is about as close as we can come to spot-on predictions. Commodity traders watch the weather, political events, and the latest consumer trends, then take an educated guess as to what might sell high or low in future markets. Predicting world political events is like driving at night with only parking lights to see what's ahead. At the end of a history course in the 1960's under British historian, Arnold Toynbee, a student asked the famous professor what he predicted for the future of Africa. In his answer, Toynbee avoided all specifics, saying only that he saw the possibility of great bloodshed. At that point, Africa was already a decade past colonial rule, although apartheid in South Africa was still in place. As for the future, Toynbee expected many small wars for the rest of the 20th Century.

Subsequent events proved his cautious prediction to be correct. At another time and place, my thesis advisor in International Relations was asked what he saw ahead in world politics. He simply replied, "I'm pessimistic about the future."

The fall of the Berlin Wall caught most of us off guard.

In 1988, when I was clandestinely teaching in ultra-oppressive Romania, I assumed I would never be able to fly into Bucharest, Budapest, Prague, and Warsaw and do what I was doing in those countries. But in hindsight, cracks in the communist system were already beginning to show up. After an evening of teaching, my 26-year-old Romanian interpreter committed an act of civil disobedience by entertaining me in his home. He told me that the Securitate, the Romanian secret police, had asked him to be an informer in his church. He said he refused. When his father learned of the request, he said, "Son, you should be more fearful." In that summer, as I also was teaching a group from another Iron Curtain country, a medical student said, "We ought not to be so afraid of the government." It was apparent that those in their 20s were deciding to stand up to their all-powerful governments.

It was in the 1980s that Soviet Premier Mikhail Gorbachev dramatically altered Soviet foreign policy to allow the Soviet satellite countries of Central and

Eastern Europe more political self-determination than any previous Soviet leader had done. Gorbachev also made major adjustments inside the Soviet Union by establishing the ground-breaking policies of *perestroika,* which called for reforms within the ruling Communist Party and restructuring of the economy, and *glasnost,* which called for democratic reforms and greater openness and transparency in the operations of the government. U.S. President Ronald Reagan loved to joke about the Soviet system, claiming he once told Mr. Gorbachev that in America any citizen can walk into his office at the White House and say, "President Reagan, I don't like the way you are running America." Gorbachev, he said, claimed it was exactly the same in the Soviet Union. "Any Russian citizen is totally free to walk into my office in the Kremlin and say, 'Premier Gorbachev, I don't like the way President Reagan is running America." All jokes aside, President Reagan delivered a bold, blunt challenge to Mr. Gorbachev during an historic speech in Berlin. Standing at that hated structure that divided East from West, Reagan demanded, "Mr. Gorbachev, tear down this wall." The Iron Lady of Great Britain, Margaret Thatcher, and Pope John Paul II, a Polish religious leader with a focus on human rights, along with Gorbachev and Reagan rounded out that era's constellation of world leaders. With astonishing suddenness, it was their combined efforts that brought the biggest changes in European history in 150 years.

Sociologists who have studied the collapse of communist dictatorships have concluded that people do not necessarily start a revolution simply because they are severely oppressed. The revolution begins the moment they decide not to be afraid of their oppressors.

The Arab Spring also seemed to happen out of nowhere.

TV images of fearless young men and women in the Middle East fighting to throw off oppressive regimes flooded our screens throughout the Arab Spring. It was young leaders who decided not to be afraid any longer, who energized older populations to challenge oppressive leaders and their heavy-handed status quo. The uprisings of the Arab Spring and the collapse of Soviet communism, both within brief periods, confirm that even the most monumental global events cannot be predicted. Similarly, any review of our individual lives confirms that none of us can say with certainty, "This is the way our lives will turn out." And the Arab Spring has not turned out as desired.

Our ancestors would be baffled and stressed if suddenly they faced life as we know it.

A professor at the Menninger School of Psychiatry told his class that throughout most of human history change came so slowly that the most significant difference from one generation to another might be an improvement in horse harnesses. My late grandparents, who were born in the 1880s, grew up in rural areas without electricity, appliances, plumbing, automobiles, phones, radios, television, highways, and dozens of other modern conveniences. If they faced today's world, they would be functionally and emotionally immobilized, at least for the short term. In terms of our once widely shared common core beliefs, our country has gone from broadly ascribing to Judaic-Christian values and virtues to the outright devaluing of those ideals by many of the nation's most influential circles. My grandparents, like nearly everyone else in those days, were proud to have a Bible in their home, although they seldom read it and rarely went to church. I learned that the *Ten Commandments* existed when I entered first grade in the public school. All *Ten Commandments* were posted on the school bulletin board and were a memory requirement. That was the first time I heard "Thou shalt not kill" presented as a divine command for a civil society. It was also in the first grade that I learned there was something called the *Lord's Prayer*. That, too, had to be memorized.

How shocked my grandparents would be to learn that a city the size of San Francisco could be destroyed with one bomb in a suitcase. Or that a "mouse" is something other than a rodent, and now part of a "laptop." A what? They would be dumbfounded by a small device they could hold in one hand and talk to almost anyone in the world. Yet even though we now expect changes to be rapid and revolutionary, the constant barrage of new necessary adjustments can cause stress and upgrade fatigue. It isn't keeping up with the Joneses that's the issue today. It's just keeping up, period. The pace of change today creates as much uncertainty as it does optimism about what's next.

So how is the script for your life turning out?

Probably not the same as the one in your head at age 18 or 20. National and international events – recessions, wars, inventions, political changes – impact personal history significantly. Also, such individual choices as if you marry, whom you marry, what you choose as an occupation many require you to constantly alter and revise that script in years to come. We may have only limited control of the plan for our lives, but it always makes sense to be proactive in pursuing the plans we believe are right. The intrusion of unforeseen factors requires flexibility to be able to bounce back with revised plans. King David comes to mind. He was not the honored firstborn in his family, but rather the youngest son sent out alone to remote grazing land with the family's herd of sheep. He certainly would not have planned on becoming the second king of Israel. Such a thought wouldn't cross his mind. It was not even a remote possibility. But God was in charge of his script, and he became one of the greatest of all military leaders and kings in the Middle East.

The unfolding stories of our lives are based partly on our own efforts and partly on forces outside us. By facing up to each new challenge, we can fill each new chapter of our lives with good responses, even in those dark, demanding chapters we left out of the script at age 18. Life is a mix of the predictable and unpredictable, sometimes far better than we had planned, sometimes much worse.

Everyone has good days and bad days.

"When times are good, be happy; but when times are bad, consider: God has made one as well as the other. Therefore, a man cannot discover anything about his future" (Ecclesiastes 7:14). This is reality. But good days and bad days do not come in equal numbers; some people have more bad days than others, some have mostly good days. But everyone gets some of each.

High school students are often pictured as happy-go-lucky guys and gals who have the world by the tail. The truth is, they have their full share of bad days. My sister, who had just turned 16, had two fender-benders the same day soon after she got her driver's license. One happened in mid-morning while she was driving from the high school campus to a nearby stadium for drum corps practice. The other occurred on her way home after school. That day was so bad that she wanted to quit driving altogether. Wisely, our dad countered, "No, you are not going to quit driving. The car still runs. You will drive to school tomorrow. We'll repair the fenders later."

That was just a "light bad day" compared to what some high school students have experienced. Bullying and violence on high school campuses have left students with indelible mental imprints that make the so-called "happy days" of high school the worst days of their lives.

Most of us hope we can avoid the bad days, but they still happen. My worst day was Bicentennial Sunday, 1976 when my wife suddenly died only a few days before her forty-first birthday, leaving three grieving children, seven, twelve, and fourteen. I wondered for a long time if I could ever be happy again, but gradually I discovered that it was possible to re-engage in life, reconstruct it, and find enjoyment, though on different terms. You, too, are likely to recall personal losses and pain, but you should not doubt the possibility of having a good life because of your particular limitations and burdens or because of bad things that happened to you. Instead, I urge you to take positive steps that lead in the direction of a good life in spite of any dark feelings you may be going through. We may never fully forget our bad days, but we can choose not to dwell on them. Keep a diary of the good times, review them occasionally, and give thanks to God and to others for those good days.

I have chosen to highlight only a few of the "givens of life," but *Ecclesiastes* has others well worth contemplating and applying.

Reflections:

1 - Since bad days can lead to pessimism and discouragement, how do you cope with this tendency in all of us, and where did this strength in you come from?

2 - What was your behavior like, and how would people around you be aware of the good and bad days?

3 - Describe one of the worst days in your life, and what led up to that day. Then describe one of the best days of your life.

CHAPTER 9
DIVERSIFY YOUR GENEROSITY AND RISKS WITH DISCERNMENT

"Cast your bread upon the waters, for after many days you will find it again. Give portions to seven, yes to eight, for you do not know what disaster may come upon the land"
(Ecclesiastes 11:1, 2).

Generosity pays off in unexpected ways.

An American family living in China during the Boxer Rebellion had practiced indiscriminate generosity with nationals for several years, giving as much as they could to any family that needed help. When foreigners suddenly had to hide for their safety, one of the poorest families of that area whom they had helped offered to take them in. The tiny house of an impoverished family turned out to be one of the safest hiding places in the town since government officials never suspected such a poor family would even know foreigners, much less be able to help them. The generous gifts of the Americans to that family "returned to them later." Their prior generosity saved their lives.

Events in life are such that people in positions of strength who have made a habit of being generous can unexpectedly find themselves among the most needy and vulnerable. Indiscriminate giving has a strange way of yielding unexpected benefits.

"It is more blessed to give than to receive" (*Acts 20:35*). Giving is part of human nature, as natural as breathing. We are made in the image of God; when we give we reflect God's characteristic of being an abundant giver. *"Every good and perfect gift is from above, coming down from the Father of heavenly lights..."* (*James 1:17*). We give food for the hungry, clothing for the ill-clad, shelter for the homeless, medicine for the ill, and comfort for those suffering to ease the messiness of this world. We instinctively know that many deficits in this life can be ameliorated by acts of generosity. Giving also keeps our hearts in a good place, because *"Wherever your treasure is, there your heart will be also"* (*Matthew 6:21*). Sharing with others to meet human need is also an act of trust that God can and will continue to give us what we need, when we need it, plus more for continued generosity.

Giving is more than writing checks or transferring funds.

Financial contributions are essential for relief and development in the world's impoverished regions and backward communities. However, hands-on volunteerism is an equally critical part of helping those areas, whether building homes with Habitat for Humanity or delivering medical supplies with such organizations as Medical Teams International, based in Portland,

Oregon. The volunteers of that organization serve people in 70 countries who are afflicted by disaster, conflict, and poverty, bringing desperately needed medical, dental, and humanitarian aid. International Relief Teams, based in San Diego, California, has been engaged in similar work, both at home and abroad, for the last 25 years. These are just a few expressions of practical generosity and dividing your generosity among many individuals and groups.

When we think of meeting people's basic needs, we usually think of food, clothing, medicine, and housing, providing things that people cannot do for themselves. An equally critical part of giving is the training and education that can only be done by volunteers who are willing to engage with people directly, and often over an extended period of time. Such training can include teaching a villager how to manage a micro-business, how to use better farming methods, and how to read and write. Doctors can donate their specialized skills by performing surgeries on those unable to pay. Health professionals can work miracles for people living in isolated and impoverished areas of the world, and some stay to teach nationals how to offer better medical care for their own communities. These many acts of compassion are just a few examples of the full range of "giving" that we can do for other people.

Giving enriches the lives of volunteers.

A physician who went to Asia to treat people with leprosy, whose nerves in their extremities were deadened and decayed, gained an unexpected appreciation for the blessing of pain. Disfigured fingers and terribly burned hands were common among leprous patients. Unable to feel pain, they often unknowingly did themselves great harm. At night, rats would chew off a sleeping victim's finger, who wouldn't even know it until morning. The physician's encounter with these horrific conditions left him with a deep understanding of the great value of the special pain sensors in our hands and feet. Pain, he realized, is God's gift to help us protect ourselves. He returned home to America with a far more profound insight into life than those who never venture beyond their comfort zones into such demanding volunteer experiences.

The spirit of giving spans all of one's activities.

Blood banks depend on volunteers both to give blood and to help operate the blood banks. Every time you give blood, you help save a life. It turns out that people who give money to charities, churches, and arts organizations are also far more likely to give blood than those who never or rarely give to such organizations.[2]

Sadly, the modern shift in values is a moving away from giving toward extreme individualism and narcissism.

The fallout from this self-centered "me-ism" is the decline both in financial contributions to non-profit organizations and in personal engagement in helping others. Many observers of contemporary society agree that the modern rise of narcissism, with its strong focus on self-love, does not bode well for future generosity.

Generosity is also thwarted when the misguided acts of giving individuals or the unintended consequences of government policies create unnecessary dependency, thus undermining people's determination to help themselves. Unwise approaches to helping others may create power for the "givers and helpers," but destroy the incentives and weaken the self-respect of those who receive such help. The possibility of healthy inter-dependent relationships does not develop in that context. Dependency relationships can also easily degenerate into oppressive relationships, the opposite of what is desirable in a healthy, reciprocal alliance of giving and receiving. This dysfunctional condition was common in societies governed by communist dictators. The government first became the sole benefactor of a population, making the people passive dependents upon that government, which then eventually became the people's controller and oppressor. I saw this sad phenomenon many times in my work with people behind the Iron Curtain.

The biblical core value is to care first for one's own family, then wider circles.

The key to grasping the scope of ideal indiscriminate biblical generosity is to accurately answer the question, *"Who is my neighbor?"* A religious leader asked Jesus this question. He was a scholar who knew that the Law of Moses declared, *"You shall love your neighbor as yourself."* Jesus answered the question of *who* with his story of the Good Samaritan. A Jewish man was traveling on a dangerous, isolated stretch of the road from Jerusalem to Jericho. Hoodlums attacked and robbed him, stripped him of his clothes and left him half dead at the side of the road. A Jewish priest saw the man but ignored his plight. He crossed over to the other side of the road and passed him by. A bit later a temple assistant did the same thing. Then came a despised Samaritan who took pity on him, rescued him, and paid for his lodging and medical care until he recovered. The ethnic hatred between Jews and Samaritans of that day was intense, but Jesus used this story to demonstrate how compassion fosters generosity and overrides the hostile differences that separate people. This timeless lesson recorded in *Luke 10:25-37* teaches that anyone who needs my help is my neighbor.

Diversification reduces economic risk.

Long ago, Asian merchants transported their products by deliberately loading their cargo into several ships. That way, if a storm sank one of the ships or pirates captured one vessel, only a part of their products was lost. Today, wise investors use the same principle by creating diverse portfolios with various mixes of mutual funds, dividend paying stocks, annuities, bonds, certificates of deposit, real estate, precious metals, and other investments, such as art, coins, and jewels. Wise investors avoid overexposure to a single industry to insulate themselves from downturns or market fluctuations. In the global economy, they may diversify even further with investments in both developed and developing economies. But whatever they do, they always follow the simple but sound principle of not putting all their eggs in one basket.

Many investors made the mistake of over-investing in Silicon Valley's high-tech start-ups, leading up to the "dot.com crash" in early 2000. Some suffered irreparable loss. They lost both their investments and their livelihoods as the companies they worked for went under. Suddenly unemployed with nothing but worthless stock options, many lost their high-priced homes, their expensive leased cars, and the chance ever to earn a comparable salary or have a secure financial future. They had to rebuild from scratch. The lessons from that debacle have led to a conscious effort in the Silicon Valley to diversify and reduce the extreme vulnerability that imperiled so many people back in 2000. Individuals, once badly burned, have been far more careful in choosing their investments.

Cities and towns that depend on one industry are at risk.

Mining towns are among those very likely to become ghost towns. These hollowed-out towns dotted the landscape in southwest Missouri and southeastern Kansas after the thriving era of iron ore mining ended. A few of those towns, like Joplin, Missouri, were able to diversify their economic bases and survive. The California Gold Rush in the eastern foothills of Sacramento triggered the rapid growth of towns like Nevada City and Grass Valley. The gold is mostly gone, but people in their golden years from the San Francisco Bay Area have turned those towns into popular retirement communities.

Detroit was once a mighty center of auto production, but that giant of the U.S. industry stumbled and fell when it was overtaken by the popularity of foreign imports and the cheaper costs of labor elsewhere. With little to take the place of making autos, Detroit has literally become a mere ghost of its prosperous past.

To limit risk of losing top leadership, a company's key leaders should not fly on the same plane.

Tesla Motor Company lost three high ranking employees when their plane crashed in Palo Alto in February 2010, creating a loss of skills and expertise that could not be easily replaced. It was one of the worst days in Tesla history. In addition to the huge emotional toll on a company, research and development teams can face massive rebuilding challenges when key members are all lost in such an accident. Vital projects can stall and collapse without the leadership that first created them.

Husbands and wives with small children often wisely fly on different planes.

Years ago, among our relatives a couple died in a plane crash and left behind two sons under age eight. Fortunately, their mother's sister and husband, with two of their own sons about the same age, took the boys into their family. But the grieving of the extended family was long and difficult. Some risks are not worth taking.

Diversity of crops protects against total loss on the farm.

Plant disease, insects, droughts and floods are common causes of crop failures. Also, repeatedly growing only one kind of crop, called "mono-cropping," depletes the soil and increases the risk of maximum loss if that one crop fails. Further, the possibility of famine rises if the food supply depends mainly on one crop.

"Sow your seed in the morning, and at evening let not your hands be idle, for you do not know which will succeed, whether this or that, or whether both will do equally well" (Ecclesiastes 11:6).

The eighteenth century Irish potato famine is a stark example of the dangers of depending on one crop. Furthermore, the Irish grew only one variety of potato, one that lacked genetic variability, as the primary source of food for the nation's poor. As the disease of potato blight spread throughout Europe, it was doubly devastating to Ireland due to the lack of diversity of the potatoes that could have been grown there. Tragically, the only variety grown in Ireland was especially susceptible to the blight. The best estimates are that at least one million people died in the famine and a million more left Ireland to try to escape it. Ireland's population was reduced by 20% or more.

Here in America, the consequences of mono-cropping hit corn growers in the Mid-West during the 2012 summer drought. At planting time, the weather looked promising. The estimate for that season's corn crop was a hefty 166 bushels per acre. By November, however, the yield came in far less than expected in what was one of the worst droughts in that region in 25 years. But in that same year, sorghum production saw a considerable increase over the year before.

Farmers in Nebraska who include sorghum in their planting as part of their crop diversification policy came through in much better shape than those who planted only corn. Sorghum needs less water and stores it more efficiently than corn. Sorghum also has a high yield of grain for each plant.

Crop diversity is essential for long-term agricultural success because repeatedly planting just one kind of crop depletes the nutrients in the soil and leaves the land literally exhausted. By rotating crops, those vital nutrients are replaced and the soil is replenished. Alfalfa and clover are excellent alternate crops because they rebuild the soil, they resist pests, they reduce weeds, and, when plowed under, they turn into "green manure."

Crop diversity helps contain erosion.

On farms with variations in the lay of the land, the long-term productivity of the soil is protected by planting crops that limit erosion on steep slopes. Minnesota farmers in one region plant alfalfa in the sloping sections of their farms to prevent erosion and plant corn in areas where the land already has adequate drainage.

Diversity Wins.

Diversity is a smart defensive strategy in the game of life to protect us from loss. It is also a wise offensive tactic to achieve the goals that lead to success.

Diversification is an important life-principle that should be applied in many dimensions of life.

Reflections:

1 - How do you go about assessing what risks to take in life? And what experiences in life have you had that influence that?

2 - Too much risk, although exciting, can be harmful. How do you go about keeping that from happening?

3 - In what ways have you practiced diversity in generosity or risks, and what have been the outcomes?

CHAPTER 10
START A GOOD LIFE WHILE YOUNG

"Be happy, young man, while you are young, and let your heart give you joy in the days of your youth. Follow the ways of your heart and whatever your eyes see, but know that for all of these things God will bring you to judgment. So then, banish anxiety from your heart and cast off the troubles of your body, for youth and vigor are meaningless. Remember the creator in the days of your youth, before the days of trouble come and the years approach when you will say, 'I find no pleasure in them.'" (Ecclesiastes 11:9-12:1).

Enjoy your youth.

Encouragement to "enjoy your youth" is the opening piece of happy advice that *Ecclesiastes* gives to young people. But that advice is set against the sober backdrop of the inevitable loss of life's enjoyment as the body grows old, breaks down, and ceases to function properly.

Youth are naturally fun-loving. Much of what constitutes the enjoyment of life, health, vigor, and optimism, is a normal part of being young. At any age, it is good to identify those attributes and to integrate them as far as possible into our own lives.

Youth are adventurous.

Daring, adventurous impulses, if exercised when one is young, can endure for a lifetime. The thrill of new discoveries, the possibilities of fame and fortune, the lure of personal growth, the willingness to take risks, make sacrifices, and even accept failure in one's quests are always vital parts of the adventurous spirit. It is this spirit that keeps us youthful at any age.

Today, young people are global in their adventures. They bike across Europe, explore the jungles of the Amazon, trek the trails and mountains of Asia, go on archaeological digs in the Middle East, and on trips to help needy people groups in the world's farthest, darkest corners. Here in America, you find youth camping in the Catskills, exploring the giant Redwoods, hiking the full length of the Appalachian Trail in the East and the Pacific Crest Trail in the West. Everywhere they are pressing beyond old limits, pushing past old boundaries, and shattering old records.

My spirit of adventure was ignited by my high school music teacher, T. Frank Coulter, and his wife who bought a tent and a bright red canoe and spent their summers camping and fishing on the lakes of Canada. Their adventures inspired me to join college friends in summertime adventures in Canada, exploring Alberta's ancient dinosaur sites and trekking British Columbia near the headwaters of the mighty Columbia River. We camped along the banks of the

St. Lawrence River, pitched our tents in the forests of New Brunswick, and basked in the outdoor quiet of Prince Edward Island.

I didn't realize it at the time, but these summers formed within me a life-long love of serious travel and high-risk adventure that prepared me for the exciting work I was called to do 25 years later behind the Iron Curtain at the height of the Cold War.

Parents, I urge you to nurture your children's spirit of adventure. Encourage your sons and daughters to plunge into new experiences. Do so while you can still supervise them, minimize any real dangers, and help guide them safely through the "danger zone" years of 16 to 24. Introduce them early on to Mark Twain's old classics, *Huckleberry Finn* and *Tom Sawyer*, which have triggered the spirit of adventure in many generations. Encourage them to try new sports, play musical instruments, go on field trips, and taste new foods. Sampling exotic food is one of the least practiced adventures by most people, young and old. Your taste buds can teach you so much about the world. Latin America, China, India, Eastern Europe, and the Middle East are just a menu away.

Youth are naturally curious.

Youth are the first to research new products and try new devices. They like to master how a thing works and what it can do. They often figure out a complicated new product the same day they buy it. This is a wonderful trait. Persistent curiosity has given us the light bulb, the airplane, radio, television, and global connectivity. Children's science fairs encourage this very kind of exploration, often setting the stage for even more discoveries.

Youth are naturally forward looking.

High school students see graduation as just the start of what's next. They are always naturally pushing forward. It's good to fully enjoy the present moment, but is vital to always be looking ahead. *Ecclesiastes* warns about getting stuck in looking back in useless longing for so-called better times of former days. It says, *"Do not say, 'Why were the old days better than these?' For it is not wise to ask such questions"* (*Ecclesiastes 7:10*). Norman Rockwell would have painted *The Good Old Days* as five old codgers sitting idly on a bench in front of a country store talking about the past. Today they meet at a "Denny's" for morning coffee.

The Apostle Paul sets a very different example. Even as he was entering old age, he made it clear that his approach to life was never to get stuck in the past. In his letter to a group of Christians in the Greek city of Philippi, he wrote, *"Forgetting what is behind and straining toward to what is ahead, I press on"* (*Philippians 3:13-14*). If we park in the past, satisfied with prior successes or paralyzed by past failures, we self-sabotage our own futures.

During a visit to a psychiatric center, I saw a statement painted on the wall almost identical to Paul's words cited above. Those words were deliberately posted there to encourage forward thinking as a powerful pathway to recover and maintain true mental health. It's no wonder that many mental health therapists call the Apostle Paul's brief letter to the Philippians the mental health document of the *New Testament.*

The practical fact is, no matter how old we are, it is both helpful and healthful to think often in a positive way about "what's next." This practice helps give purpose and direction to our lives. Moses was 80 years old when he was summoned by God to deliver his fellow Hebrews from their Egyptian masters, liberating them from slavery and shaping them into a free nation under God. The epic life of Moses fired the imagination of 20th Century Hollywood, resulting in the classic film *The Ten Commandments,* with mega-star Charlton Heston in the lead role.

It was the most radical kind of forward thinking that has enabled the so-called Silicon Valley of California's San Francisco Bay Area to become the high-tech capital of the world. Young, adventurous, "next thinking" engineers pioneered the astonishing rise of such high-tech titans as Hewlett Packard, Microsoft, Intel, and Apple. Apple's Steve Jobs created new products right to the end of his all too brief life, transforming entire industries in the process. Next, the new wave of the young and restless ushered in our new era of Google, Facebook, and all their mass communication cousins.

I've often pondered about the forward looking thinking of another country, Poland. What is it about Poland's culture and parenting and community encouragement that has given the world Copernicus in revolutionary astronomy, Chopin in timeless music composition, Paderewski in matchless piano performances, Pope John Paul II in global religious influence, and Lech Walesa in the fearless leadership of Poland's labor unions that led to the end of Communist rule over that country? Each of these outstanding Poles was creative, adventurous, and fearless, daring to go boldly where others hesitated and held back. At every age in every country, these dynamic attributes lead to far greater enjoyment of life.

Youth naturally need help in making responsible decisions.

The best foundations for making good decisions are high standards of morals and ethics linked with the habit of carefully considering how one's decisions are likely to impact one's self and others. This kind of mature decision making is a refined skill that develops gradually as children are first taught the basics of right and wrong, then given opportunities to exercise their own judgments and make their own decisions about what clothes to wear, what sports to play, what things to buy. Wide exposure to many options and frequent chances to make choices prepare young people to work through more complex situations and more difficult options. Parents and other responsible adults can offer the pros and cons of possible choices, but then entrust their sons and daughters with the freedom and the responsibility to make their own choices. This is an ideal way for youth to learn the rewards, consequences, benefits, limitations and potentials of the decisions they make.

A basic principle for teaching youth about decisions is to help them get all the information possible about the potential outcomes and likely consequences of each decision. Young people often by-pass this important process under the pressure of peer influence and the desire for peer approval.

Some decisions, of course, are far more important than others. At the top of this list is the choice of the person one marries. Young men and women ask, "How can I really know if this is the right person for me?" Powerful emotions and strong physical attraction can easily override the most important aspects of what it takes to make a good marriage. Based on my decades of observing young people make good and bad choices of marriage partners, I strongly urge young couples to go through extensive personality assessments in pre-marital counseling. At minimum, such counseling should include 7 sessions over 13 weeks. Experts say this is the least number of sessions and shortest time frame to be truly effective in identifying strengths, uncovering weaknesses, and spotting potential pitfalls for a long-term relationship. For example, suppose the counselor asks your husband-to-be what his idea of a perfect day is. If he answers, "A fishing rod in one hand and a beer in the other," you know you've got a guy who likes to have a good time in the great outdoors. If he answers, "A Bible in one hand and a catalogue of new tractors in the other," you know you are headed to a different kind of life. If she answers the same question by saying, "A trip to San Francisco to shop 'til I drop," you know you'll need a good income to finance such sprees, or she will. But if she says, "Spend the day at home, cook a huge Italian meal, and bake cookies for the kids," you know you've got a different future ahead. This is exactly the kind of information that lets you know if it's best to back off or move on in this all-important relationship.

When it comes to career decisions, such choices are easy for some because somehow they seem to know early on what they want to pursue. Some enter trade school to use their natural aptitudes in those fields they enjoy and move quickly toward well-paying jobs. Some grow up in a family business and happily follow that path. Others enroll in college with no career direction and try to figure it out as they go. This kind of searching can be a very good thing. Students with no clear vision for their future may change their majors, be exposed to many disciplines, explore many possibilities, and emerge from academia very satisfied with their college experiences and very focused on their future work.

Former U.S. Secretary of State Condoleezza Rice is a good example of the positive results of shifting majors and changing one's career focus. She enrolled at the University of Denver to study music, but she discovered her real life's passion in an elective class on International Relations. Her switch in majors set her on a career course that took her to the pinnacle of American foreign policy. By following her heart she has had an extraordinary life.

Jazz genius Dave Brubeck, like Condoleezza Rice, made a major change of direction in his college years at the University of the Pacific. He enrolled with the apparent intent to become a veterinarian. He'd grown up in rural ranch country in Northern California, so studying veterinary medicine was a natural first choice of his life's work. But under the influence of his musically London-trained mother, he was also an excellent pianist. He gradually became involved in music classes, which became the sole focus of his study and his ambitions. The rest is jazz history.

Also keep in mind that after 20 years in one field you may want to change careers to a related or even very different field. An engineer, for example might want to teach math to young people. Such a change would require only a teaching credential and familiarity with the school's math curriculum. More radical shifts in careers sometimes come from one's hobby or avocation. Julia Child had a career in government intelligence in Europe during World War II, but became a famous author and television chef by sharing her passions for the delights of French cuisine.

Some changes, of course, are urgently necessary due to circumstances that are unforeseen, unwelcome, and beyond one's control. This kind of dire necessity was forced upon the Von Trapp family when the Nazis invaded and took control of their native Austria. Nazi rule forced them to make the sudden, daring, and difficult choice to leave behind the wealthy life they'd known in order to flee tyranny in favor of freedom. Their decision inspired Rogers and Hammerstein to celebrate their courage in the timeless musical, *Sound of Music.*

In Hebrew history, King David's approach to military operations is a fine example of sound decision-making. Surrounded by hostile nations, David was forced to engage in many battles. As he dealt with these repeated challenges, a pattern of wise decisions emerged. Rather than follow rigid military policy, like many modern leaders, each time David went to war, often with a new enemy, he was keenly aware of battle conditions that were new and unknown. That awareness drove him to seek God's special direction for each unique battle. The divine guidance he received in answer to his prayers made David one of history's most successful military leaders.

Like David's battles, your life situations, though seemingly routine, are seldom exactly the same as ones you've faced repeatedly in the past. Therefore, a wise principle for taking action in any situation is to ask God for divine direction every time, asking what is to be done, when to it is to be done, and how. Also, seek the counsel of trusted people around you. Standard policies and conventional wisdom can be useful, but they can also limit your thinking and narrow your choices if you do not keep yourself open to change.

Also, the easily accessible information about daily decision-making now freely available on the Internet can be very helpful in refining the skills needed to work through complicated situations successfully. Furthermore, seeking guidance from a professional counselor can help insure you have turned every stone before making your final decision on significant issues. Finally, it is always advisable to filter all decisions, large and small, through your own value system and through biblical standards of right and wrong. Always keep in mind that justice and mercy are important for everyone affected by what you decide.

Youth need to get to know God.

In anything, starting young gives you a head start. That includes developing a personal relationship with one's Maker. Following the guidelines given us by the Creator of the Universe is a sure shortcut to a good life by helping us avoid life's self-created messes. Even more important, Scripture promises that those who know God will do valiant things.

The Ten Commandments is a good place to begin. This remarkably brief yet fully comprehensive list of real life principles gives a solid framework for decisions and behaviors that create and sustain a fulfilling, well-integrated life for individuals, and a fruitful, functional life for society. Moses emphasized obeying all the commandments, including its laws, rules, and precepts, *"Observe them carefully, for this will show your wisdom and understanding to the nations, who will hear about all these decrees and say, 'Surely this great nation is a wise and understanding people.' ... What other nation is so great as to have such righteous decrees and laws as this body of laws I am setting before you today?"* (Deuteronomy 4:6-7). Each of the Ten Commandments fills a specific role in our lives, guiding us to potential positive outcomes. Contrary to much modern thinking, the Commandments do not arbitrarily limit us, nor do they detract from the full enjoyment of life. Instead, they protect and enrich our lives. They make life work like it is supposed to work.Here are some examples:

Thou shalt remember the Sabbath Day to keep it holy.

"Six days you shall labor and do all your work, but the seventh day is a Sabbath to the Lord your God" (Exodus 20:8).

The Sabbath Day is a day of rest, a satisfying gift to the world. Never forget, it is this command from God that established the pattern for our coveted weekends. The Hebrew Sabbath was Friday sundown to Saturday sundown. The Hebrews shared their practice of Sabbath observance wherever they traveled and settled throughout the world. Without their example and influence, we might well be trapped in a 24/7 cycle that begins at birth and ends only at death. Imagine never having a day off. Enjoy your restful weekends because God had this very thing in mind for you when he designed the Sabbath.

The principle of the Sabbath went beyond just one day of rest each week for the people. It also applied to the land. Land farmed by the Israelites was to be rested one year out of every seven years. In that seventh year, no crops were to be planted or harvested. The people were to store enough food to last two years. Modern science has proven the value of rest for the land. Constant planting and harvesting of the land leads to serious depletion of soil nutrients.

Ironically, today's communication technology is creating an unhealthy 24/7 life cycle. This is especially true for youth who are wired, connected, and constantly texting and posting night and day. Some college students are so addictively connected that they fail their courses and drop out of school. Truly human connections wither when one is incessantly staring at the screen of a smart phone. A person who is texting may be acting as if he is paying attention to the person he is with, even by looking into their eyes, but the person present is rarely fooled. This kind of constant distraction can leave the person present feeling diminished and resentful. All too often, people we are with physically seem to be someplace else entirely, distracted, distant, and remote. Is this really what we want? Consider taking a Sabbath rest from the dumb use of smart phones. Parents, I urge you to get your children out to see the world, show them how to engage with people, and remove them from non-stop smart phone texting, video games, and TV.

Thou shalt not steal.

If everyone kept this commandment, the integrity of each person's property would be secure. If you own property, no one would arbitrarily change or encroach upon your property line. If you leave your purse or wallet in a store, when you return to search for it, your driver's license, credit cards, and cash would all still be there. Both your money and your identity would be safe.

Though shalt not commit adultery.

This command preserves the integrity of marriage and guards the stability of family life, which is the basic building block of any sound society. Trust between mates deeply enriches their relationship. Their children feel secure, which is a proven factor in children's success in school and beyond. Children of intact, functional families are also more likely to contribute in life to the common good of society. By contrast, if adultery is common, if the devaluation of marriage is widespread, the inevitable personal and social consequences include broken families, school dropouts, increases in crime, and lower standards of living. The long-term impact may also be an almost irreversible pattern in a society's population.

In *The Song of Solomon,* another book of Wisdom Literature in the Old Testament, the enjoyment of physical intimacy of marriage is presented as a private, walled garden of shared delights, well protected from outside dangers and distractions. The male lover says of his bride, *"You are a garden locked up, my sister, my bride; you are a spring encircled, a sealed fountain"* *(Song of Solomon 4:12).*

A Stanford University professor teaching a course on "Family Trends in America" stated flatly, "Open marriages do not work." Sex outside of a marriage spoils what is inside that marriage. Modern research strongly supports those conclusions, solidly confirming the practical, pragmatic value of the Seventh Commandment.

The Old Testament prophet Nehemiah spoke strongly of the destructive consequences of ignoring God's directives. As for theft, today's threats to property are driving people into gated communities with costly security measures, which for some means high walls topped with embedded glass and razor wire and attack dogs prowling the grounds. As for Sabbath rests, ignoring that command has produced a population of people who are forever fatigued and perpetually on the brink of burnout. As for adultery, the consequences are often divorce, devastating financial setbacks, great stress and confusion in child rearing, and sometimes sexually transmitted diseases, as tragically portrayed in the motion picture *Out of Africa*.

The sad fact is, stubbornly insisting on doing it our way is a sure path to messed-up lives. Do not be fooled by the philosophy of Frank Sinatra's popular song, *I Did It My Way,* which became a motto in late 20th Century America. Billy Joel promoted radical individualism with his lyrics. Now fast forward to our 21st Century and a song by the Weezer group, *The Greatest Man That Ever Lived.* It's easy to guess who that man is. Focusing on self is not a value system upon which to build a good life, but the pervasive popularity of such music is a clear cultural indicator of the rapid rise of unrestrained narcissism.

I've highlighted three of the Ten Commandments in this chapter. The other seven are equally important, each with its modern-day applications. Together, they insure the safety, well-being, and full enjoyment of life and they form the most solid foundation for wise decision-making.

These are the high points of Solomon's writing about youth, and with little transition he moves on to describe the final years of "life under the sun."

Reflections:

1 - Is it possible to practice both justice and mercy at the same time? Why or why not? Do you know of biblical examples?

2 - How would life change if we kept one disconnected Sabbath day every week?

3 - If you've not started on a desired adventure, what's holding you back? What are the steps you need to take to "add-the-venture"?

CHAPTER 11
DON'T LET AGE GET YOU DOWN

"However many years a man may live, let him enjoy them all" *(Ecclesiastes 11:8).*

American culture is fixated on youth. Multiple touch-up plastic surgeries are now common. Fortunes are spent on hair replacement and hair colorings that promise to leave only a touch of gray. The prospect of turning 60 and entering the so-called Golden Years is frightening to many people.

Playwright Arthur Miller's brief marriage to Marilyn Monroe gave him a vantage point to observe life in Hollywood. He is reported to have said, "Life in California is like an endless voyage; people just fall overboard into a well-manicured cemetery."

Growing old calls for a review of several life issues.

It's a mistaken assumption that people get better as they get older. The truth is, the older set has its own vulnerabilities to sinful temptations and to senior delinquency. Think back to the time of your youth and take a good look at the types of temptations you faced. Now look at how those same temptations take on different forms in later life.

French philosopher Jean-Jacques Roseau developed a table of sequential temptations according to one's age. A boy of 10, he said, is tempted by a cake. A young man of 20 by a girl. A man of 30 by pleasure. A man of 40 by success. A man of 50 by avarice, the accumulation of wealth. Roseau had it just about right. Convicted swindler Bernard Madoff and Enron executives, lost in their pursuit of money, were all over 50.

I don't know why Roseau stopped at 50. Perhaps it was because life spans in his day were much shorter and death for most people age 50 was just around the corner. I think it is now necessary to add at least one more age-specific temptation for those who are in the category of 65-plus. Their special temptation is *entitlement*. In fact, perhaps the older generation should be labeled the entitled generation. Entitled to what?

During a retirement party, a woman made a comment to me that she knew could be considered improper by some of the guests. She then said, "I guess at our age we can say anything we want to." Not wanting to dash cold water on her evening, I merely uttered, "perhaps." After that incident, I began to listen more carefully to the conversations of my contemporaries. I observed that she was not alone in her attitude. Many seem to think that advancing age gives one the right to say or do just about anything they want. Many modern movies and television programs dealing with the behavior of older people reinforce that attitude. Ornery, irascible, profane, vulgar, tactless old coots, men and women, are celebrated as senior role models.

This presumption of entitlement is captured in a contemporary birthday card. The picture on the front shows an old, white, plump-bellied cat stretched out on a posh living room chair, eyes closed, sound asleep. Next to the cat, he is cradling a partially eaten piece of three-layer yellow cake with bright pink icing. Half dangling from his paw is a dessert fork with pink icing. The seven-word greeting inside the card reads: "You are not spoiled. You are entitled."

This attitude, "I'm entitled," easily crescendos into "I deserve," then "I demand." That's when life can turn very ugly for old people and for the people around them.

Advancing age requires increasing moderation.

No matter how we feel about growing old, everyone who lives long enough gets there. Time takes care of that. A key to creating both a long life and a good life requires conscious effort to make some tough decisions and carry out those decisions with sustained discipline. I think of chocolate as a metaphor for growing older and enjoying life simultaneously. Chocolate tastes wonderful. It's even good for us if consumed in moderation. Moderation is the key. Too much chocolate can lead to an early death. A woman I knew kept a five-pound box of chocolates on her coffee table. During one of my visits, she said, "Pass the chocolates, I'm weak." She died far younger than necessary, her body bloated by over-indulgence. As we age, we need to practice more moderation in everything.

A retired research physician says, "I believe the body is built to last 100 years."

He made that comment during one of his regular workouts at the gym. Things that work against such optimal longevity include unhealthy life styles, accidents, diseases for which there are as yet no known cures, and lack of proper dental or medical care. Even so, I've known people who did live that long and enjoyed a good life to the very end. So it's possible.

Solomon thought a lot about longevity. He addresses the issue of death early in *Ecclesiastes*, but he holds off on painting the detailed picture of old age until the last chapter. There, his description of man in old age reads like the bad results of an annual checkup when you are too far gone to drive to the doctor's office by yourself. Here's a brief, modern paraphrase of the list of everything that Solomon says can go downhill at that time of life: cataracts that cloud the eyes, knees and hips that need replacement, dentures to replace decayed teeth, ears that don't hear without the aid of some $6,000 hearing device, sex as a fading memory, a voice that shakes when you speak and quivers when you try to sing, steps and inclines that seem like mountain slopes, and stringy white hair, followed by a scarcely attended funeral and maybe a tiny obituary in some newspaper, read by almost no one.

Also, most people living past 90 have lost most of their friends. A church in California was packed to the walls for the funeral of a prominent woman who died in her early 70s. As people filed out, a much older woman was overheard saying to her friend, "When you're in your 70s, you can still draw a good crowd, but by the time you're in your 80s, like us, most people don't remember you or aren't well enough to attend the service."

My mother, who died at 97, had only one living friend in her age group. Even so, she had two generations of younger friends who gladly showed up to celebrate her 96th birthday party.

Decline and loss are part of old age. Travel is more difficult, but that did not stop Mrs. Fisher, mentioned earlier, to enjoy a perk of turning 100 by using a free one-hundredth birthday pass by United Airlines to fly from Denver to Seattle to visit her cousin.

Fortunately, physical functions tend to decline gradually rather than suddenly. Most people can therefore adjust in an orderly manner. The challenge is how to keep life well rounded through the period of inevitable decline, which can last 10, 15, 20 years. A British physician remarked, "After age 55, everybody is a bit crumbly." If he's right, the challenge is what do we do between 55 and 85 or longer.

At 55, or even a few years sooner, it's a good time to have a value check and to identify any important unfulfilled goals.

My interactions with college students have convinced me that some of them have goals and values based on the principles of altruism. They want to live out the biblical principles of loving their neighbors as themselves, practicing justice, and showing mercy. But it is easy to become tired in the pursuit and practice of such ideals when faced with the many obstacles that block achievement and that oppose goodness. This kind of disappointment and disillusionment is not uncommon in the 50-plus age bracket. That's why this is an important time to check one's self for value slippage in this and other areas of life.

Unfulfilled goals can be unsettling and lead to cynicism about life. In the previous chapter, I mentioned the challenge a college professor gave us about looking five, ten, fifteen or twenty years ahead and deciding what we hoped to accomplish. He also stressed annual reviews of those goals to be sure we were doing what it takes to achieve them. The mid-50s in life is another good time to do a serious review of one's goals and to determine if it's time to alter them or to pursue them with fresh vigor.

Assuming you have done a good job of forming your goals and values, the new challenge is to manage the limitations imposed by the decline that accompanies old age. Make a point to identify good role models in this age group. I think of a couple approaching their 70's who made a 35-mile move to the small Missouri town where their son-in-law practiced medicine. They chose a home just two miles across town from their daughter where they could easily be helped if needed. But they also made sure they were not living on top of each other or intruding in unwanted ways into their daughter's family life. Within three years of that move, he died. She lived 25 years longer. In her mid-80's, she had a small house built next to her daughter, just in case she needed more support. Soon after that, her son-in-law retired, but was shortly diagnosed with cancer. During the difficult time that he was dying, she was the one nearby to help her daughter. Finally in her early 90's she moved in with her daughter and lived for another five years. Only in the very last part of that five-year period did she have to go to a full care facility. This couple always stayed ahead of the game. It helped them and their family to have good lives.

I once asked a pastor of senior adults his advice for dealing with physical decline. He said, "I always encourage older persons to make the next move before they have to." That way, he said, they always keep better control of their lives. He applied that principle to his own situation, saying: "I'm going to Southern California next week to help my mother move into her own small apartment in an assisted living facility. My wife and I convinced her that if she made the move now, she could decide what paintings, furniture, and items she wanted to take with her." He convinced her that if she waited too long, he would have to make those decisions for her. Also, he helped her understand that she would have more social interaction there and, while she was still reasonably strong, she could easily adjust and build new relationships.

A few years ago, a dirt bike enthusiast and I were discussing the aging process when he commented that he had recently decided to reduce his riding area from 11,000 acres down to 6,000 acres of land south of Silicon Valley. He still enjoyed the sport, but at a more manageable level. A few years later, he wisely recognized it was time to quit altogether. He cleaned up the equipment, loaded it in his pickup, and passed it on to his grandson, who is now perpetuating his legacy of love for the sport. Though no longer on the dirt bike, he has great photos of wonderful escapades with his buddies.

Physical decline is real, and that necessitates adjustments.

Some years ago, a San Francisco Bay Area pathologist led a study of longevity immunology in San Francisco and three European cities. He discovered that the immune system of the average person begins a steady decline in the early 60's. By age 85, the effective immune level drops low enough for cancer, pneumonia, and other diseases to easily take hold. The results of this study should prompt seniors to stay alert to even slight changes in health status and to be immunized against shingles and pneumonia.

Older persons often make the common and costly mistake of delaying treatment for what they think are minor medical issues that don't demand immediate care. Then, before they realize it, one or two additional problems emerge. Quality of life can then go into a medical tailspin. The solution is simple: don't ignore minor medical problems. Get proper treatment as soon as possible. You will be better off, and so will your adult children.

Transitioning from late middle age into old age can be as tricky and confusing as getting through adolescence. When I turned 60, I thought, "How do I refine my plans should I die in the next three years or live another 30? At 60, in 120 months I would be 70. In 240 months, 80. That's not like being 20 when it's natural to project 40 years into the future."

When older, just like in the teenage years, changes occur quickly.

Unlike teenagers who usually stay healthy and become stronger, changes for those over 60 go in the opposite direction. Therefore, contingency planning is in order, but I suggest moving forward and anticipating a good future. Many people have productive, enjoyable lives through their 70's, 80's and 90's. Secretary of State Henry Kissinger is still productive and actively involved in foreign policy issues beyond 90. President H.W. Bush made his last parachute jump at age 90.

Groups of older people can greatly help each other by taking time to talk about how they are managing issues of aging, especially if they don't turn the session into a time of jokes and complaints about aches and pains.

I've asked many older people about their philosophy of growing old. They've given me some helpful ideas about how best to manage it. At 55, a retired professor said, "I pondered what kind of person I wanted to be if I lived to 80. I decided I had better live that way today because I've observed that old people seem to become more so of what they were when they were younger."

"Every year," said another retired professor, "it seems to take longer and longer to do less and less. I now space my activities more carefully than I used to."

"Keep learning something new," said a retired Army chaplain. "I'm learning to text. Otherwise I would not be able to communicate with my grandchildren and hopefully influence them through their college years."

A San Francisco area physician advises people planning to retire within the next ten years. "If you want to stay out of the rest home, it's legs, legs, legs." He was still running marathons after age 75. Health care professionals also stress proper nutrition and weight control—eating right and staying active. The old adage says, "A lean horse for a long run."

For older clients, a top-flight gym trainer in Silicon Valley who was a former Soviet Union national wrestling coach, emphasizes flexibility and strength. "After 55, it's weights, weights, weights," he says, "and 30 minutes of stretching every day." I'm stressing physical well-being here because the most obvious characteristic of aging is physical decline. Without reasonable health, such life basics as productivity, enjoyment of each day, and contributing to others is very limited, if not impossible.

The mind and the heart need as much attention as our bodies.

Scripture reassures us that God does not abandon the old, and that age need not be a hindrance for a productive life. The Apostles Peter and Paul both were older and active until martyred. Moses was between 80 and 120 when he accepted and carried out the challenge of building a stable and thriving society. Those leaders did not express a hint of entitlement. Quite the opposite. Toward the end of his life, Paul wrote: *"I have learned to be content whatever the circumstances. I know what it is to be in need, and I know what it is to have plenty. I have learned the secret of being content in any and every situation, whether well fed or hungry, whether living in plenty or in want"* (*Philippians 4:11, 12*). The Old Testament prophet Isaiah wrote about God's care for us. *"Even to your old age and gray hairs I am he, I am he who will sustain you. I have made you and I will carry you; I will sustain you and I will rescue you" (Isaiah 46:4). "But those who hope in the Lord will renew their strength. They will soar on wings like eagles; they will run and not grow weary, they will walk and not be faint"* (Isaiah 40:31).

An excellent example of turning 70 with an exceptionally clear view of how best to move ahead is captured in an excerpt from a letter friend Len Sunukjian sent to many of us when he reached the 70-year milestone. I met Len nearly 40 years ago when he was a leader on the staff of Mount Hermon Conference Center, near Silicon Valley. He continues to radiate the noble aspirations which keep life meaningful to the very end, and he always knew how *"to make everything beautiful in its time."* He titled his letter:

"What's Ahead?"

"So what's ahead? *Psalm 92:12-14* charts my desired course to FINISH WELL. *'But the godly will flourish like palm trees and grow strong like the cedars of Lebanon. For they are transplanted into the Lord's own house. They flourish in the courts of our God. Even in old age they will still produce fruit; they will remain vital and green.'*

"Finishing well is characterized by flourishing in the community of God's people and continuing in fruitful ministry as one ages. A few years ago my wife and I vacationed in Idaho. On one of our hikes I came across this sign on a tree: 'I was hollow long before I died.'

'Lord, have mercy on me. I want to stay fresh and green... not hollow and dead.'

"I enjoy reading Louis L'Amour, who is regarded as America's Favorite Storyteller, with more than 225 million copies of his books in print around the world. In one of his full-time Westerns, *The Californios,* Juan, the Old One, says to a younger man, *'All men age, as all men die. The thing is not to die too soon and to live wisely. To live a long time is nothing: to live a long time wisely is something.'* Regardless of how much longer I live here on earth, I want to live wisely now... knowing I'm going to live forever. How about you?"

Aging well with God in our lives is summarized by the Apostle Paul in plain, realistic, and universally understood terms: *"Though our bodies are dying, our spirits are being renewed every day... (and) the joys to come will last forever"* (2 Corinthians 4:16, 18).

Reflections:

1 - Have you done your annual life review? What is going well and what is not going well in your physical, relational, and spiritual life?

2 - Do you have a mentor, spiritual adviser, friend, or accountability group to hold you accountable for your review? Was this one of the reasons for Solomon's downfall? What could he have done differently?

3 - What do you want to sustain, improve, or correct in your life? What action steps are necessary to be where you want to be? Are they scheduled, and are you following through?

CHAPTER 12
HOLD LIFE TOGETHER
WITH GOD

"Teach me how to live, O Lord" (Psalm 27:11).

Many benefits are ours when we focus on God and keep him at the center of life.

As Roberto and I drove through *rancho pobre* country in Oaxaca, Mexico we did our best to absorb the beauty of a lavender canopy of jacaranda trees in full bloom as they covered the narrow highway. Lush valleys of lettuce and other crops lay just beyond the trees, but most of the inhabitants there had none of life's amenities, and few necessities. However, the community we visited was an exception. Roberto had cultivated spiritual renewal by introducing them to biblical principles for creating a better life. He encouraged them to sustain their hard work that began at sun up and continued until early afternoon when their wives brought lunch to them in the fields, and then resumed work until sundown. He urged them to stop wasteful spending on mistresses and Saturday-night drinking parties, but rather, invest their energy, enjoyment, and income into their families. With more money in their pockets, they built better homes and provided adequate food and clothing for their children.

They were now living satisfied lives. What a sharp contrast between their past and the present.

Roberto also brought hybrid lettuce seed from California and showed them how to prepare the harvested produce for more profitable export. They were grateful that he had guided them to a better life through sharing his agricultural skills along with biblical ideas for managing life.

Living God's way consistently raises standards of *"life under the sun."*

This reality became visible just months before communist rule collapsed in the Soviet Union. When I was teaching for a couple of weeks near the Black Sea in the spring of 1990, the institute director took me for a short outing to observe a newly formed enterprise by the local Christian Business Men's Association. Under Michael Gorbachev, *perestroika* and *glasnost* gave entrepreneurs and capitalist oriented Russians a bit of elbow room to start small businesses. The institute director commented, "You will notice that all ten employees are working and the boss is not even here." That was unusual because in state-owned operations workers often lolled around on the job, turned out shoddy products and sometimes went to movies on company time. My question was, "What made the difference?" He replied, "It's simple. The owners of the business pay them four times as much as the government. And their products are in high demand because of the high quality." Application of biblical principles, in this case, "treat people right" and "pursue excellence in all things," leads to a better life.

All human beings have equal worth.

In an earlier and radically different setting in the 1960's when British historian, Arnold Toynbee, was visiting professor at the University of Denver, he commented when discussing the global issues of racism and nationalism, "Missionaries are among the few people in the world who overcome racism and nationalism." His statement in the history class did not appear to be an effort to promote missionary activity nor exalt missionaries, but rather just an observation he had made as a student of cultures and world history. Believing that all races are created equal, should be treated equally, and that God is the God of all nations, curbs inclinations to behave in a prejudiced or discriminatory way toward groups other than one's own.

In the first century, St. Paul applied the biblical mandate that everyone is to be accepted and treated impartially. He wrote to Christians living in what is now modern day Turkey, *"There is neither Jew nor Gentile, slave nor free, male nor female for you are all one in Christ Jesus" (Galatians 3:27).* Centuries later in England William Wilberforce echoed a conviction that all human beings are equal and worthy of equal treatment. He engaged in a political battle as the voice of the abolition movement in the British Parliament, and eventually, after many years, won that battle. The movie, *Amazing Grace,* is the wonderful story of his life, struggles, and achievement in eliminating slavery. Whenever and wherever God's directives are practiced, racism, nationalism, sexism and ethnic conflict are ameliorated and often eliminated.

In Solomon's day most women were still living in the *Dark Ages* of women's rights. They were the property of men. Progress began in overcoming this injustice when Jesus launched respect for women during his ministry. Later, the Apostle Paul addressed this historical problem with the teaching that husbands were to love their wives as they love themselves. *"Husbands ought to love their wives as their own bodies. He who loves his wife loves himself"* (Ephesians 5:28). He also advanced the concept of mutual submission. *"Submit to one another out of reverence for Christ"* (Ephesians 5:21). *"The wife's body does not belong to her alone but also to her husband. In the same way, the husband's body does not belong to him alone, but also to his wife"* (1 Corinthians 7:4). Nothing in history matches what the Bible has done for women as equal in God's eyes.

Unified and functional communities emerge if the members of society follow the intentions of God for how we are to relate to one another. St. Paul also declared of God, *"From one man he made every nation of men"* (Acts 17:26). Therefore, all human beings are fundamentally related, though living in different climates, nations, and cultures. The founders of the United States established a motto similar to the Apostle Paul's call for unity: *"E pluribus unum – From many one."* Though not originally meant to address cultural and racial diversity, if implemented even imperfectly, it is beneficial as a national goal.

A former Department of State diplomat and San Francisco State University professor, who assisted American missionaries in the process of leaving China during the Communist takeover in 1949, said that he believed Taiwan made rapid and remarkable social and economic progress in the 1950's and '60's because of the high concentration of missionaries who resettled there when they could no longer work in China. Taiwan benefitted substantially from their influence and work.

Keeping God at the center of life also gives meaning and purpose at the individual level. Thousands of people who felt empty found life worth living after they read Rick Warren's book, *The Purpose Driven Life*, and decided to put it into practice. They may not have committed to a purpose as daring, sacrificial, and all-consuming as Mother Teresa's, but they quietly and privately discovered their purpose, and acted on it.

Serious handicaps and physical limitations do not stop some people from making good lives for themselves, with God's help.

They make wise and demanding choices in managing and limiting the impact of adversity, such as Joni Eareckson Tada. By not avoiding visibility, but rather by sharing her life and insight, she has been highly productive as a quadriplegic. Unafraid to ask for the support she needed, she established goals, no matter how small they may seem, gave attention to the study of the Bible and meditation, and always offered thanksgiving for blessings. She has created a challenging "stewardship of adversity" for the rest of us to consider, whatever limitations we may face. *"We also rejoice in our sufferings, because we know that suffering produces perseverance, perseverance, character, and character, hope" (Romans 5:3, 4).*

Regardless of personal circumstances, the winning mix for a good life is to keep God at the center, to fuse respect and love for Him with applications of His directives. This is a narrow path. In contrast to it, is a wide and easy road that can abruptly dead-end. That wide road is appealing. It begins as alluringly as the movie, *Days of Wine and Roses*. This tragic story begins in a San Francisco setting, so beautiful that the sight of the Golden Gate, the scent of the sea, and the impressionist images created by a light fog invite you to linger with Joe Clay and Kirsten Amesen, an engaging couple enjoying the beauty of The City, each other, and the satisfying taste of Napa Valley Merlot. But they drifted gradually and as slowly as a *largo* movement of a symphony into indulgence. Finally, into addiction, to a point beyond return. "When enough was enough" was overlooked. The warning signals were missed. *"Do not gaze at wine when it is red, when it sparkles in the cup, when it goes down smoothly! In the end it bites like a snake and poisons like a viper"* (Proverbs 23:31, 32). San Francisco and roses were no longer beautiful. And wine, only an escape. All human beings face the possibility of similar endings. The danger is always there. For that reason, *"Draw near to God, and He will draw near to you."*

When it's time to say goodbye.

As Andrea Bocelli and Sarah Brightman ended a concert singing, *Time to Say Goodbye,"* eventually the time will come for all of us when it's time to say goodbye to this earth with its sights, its sounds, and goodbye to the people we love. Some say it well; others have a terrible struggle. A close friend who died of prostate cancer did say it well. He and his wife had just retired to their native Oregon where they bought a cottage in the woods near a small town, a dream fulfilled after years of teaching in an urban area. There, they had planned a simple life mixed with some travel and lecturing, but soon after the move, he was diagnosed with terminal cancer.

On my first visit after his diagnosis, we took a three-mile walk on a forest trail and talked about life and death. "I know I'm dying," he said, "but right now I don't feel like it. It's a strange place to be." He went on, "But the doctor told me that as I begin to decline and have to deal with the pain I will gradually decide that it's time to let go."

Mid-way in the decline he commented that one of the things that bothered him most was that he could no longer be productive and engage in the lives of others. My response was, "All of your life you have been a producer. You have enriched the lives of scores of people. It's OK to be a consumer now." I learned later that this comment helped him with that issue. At the beginning of life, and often at the end, we are dependent on care given by others. Not an expectation we like to think about, but it is reality. The last time I visited him only a few weeks before his death, he said, "Now life offers so little that it is not worth the effort to stay alive." I could only reply, "That's OK." Saying goodbye hurts, but he made it a little easier by always saying it well throughout the experience.

King David, father of Solomon, knew how to say it well. Just before Solomon was anointed King of Israel, David gave him this charge, *"I am about to go the way of all the earth... so be strong, show yourself a man, and observe what the Lord your God requires. Walk in his ways, and keep his decrees and commands, his laws and requirements as written in the Law of Moses, so that you may prosper in all you do and wherever you go" (1 Kings 2:2, 3).* David soon died and was buried in Jerusalem. And life went on for the next generation as it will after each of us says goodbye.

Reflections:

1 - What do you want to be remembered for? Why? Where did you get this value in your life? Have you shared this with the key people who you want to remember your life? Are they aware of what to be looking for? What do they want to be remembered for? Have you asked them and why they have this desire? Are you honoring their request and letting them know in what ways they will be remembered? And are they giving you a response that tells you that you have in mind what they desire?

2 - How do you remember Solomon's life? Why? Does your response give you some ideas for your own life?

3 - Among the people you know or among those you have read about, who are your models for "holding life together?"

CONCLUSION:
ABOUT SOLOMON AND YOUR LIFE

At the end of Solomon's life he seemed to return to his position as a younger man by affirming that true wisdom begins with knowing God and living by His guidelines. We are accountable both before God and by those who live after us as they observe and experience our legacy. When young and strong, Solomon carelessly indulged during his "life under the sun" in many things God negates. As old age crept upon him, he could not ignore the inborn, God-created sense that life extends beyond our timeframe "under the sun." We are created to live forever. Eternity is embedded in man's mind!

As his hair grayed, he reflected on life in general and on his life in particular. He seemed to recognize that the pain and dissatisfaction he experienced were often self-generated. He also seemed to sense what would go wrong in the nation after his death was because of his personal excesses and his oppressive leadership. Old age yanked him back to the reality of what's basic and really important in life. With *Ecclesiastes,* we are the beneficiaries of his reflection and his regrets. Hopefully, with his conclusions to guide us, we will be more careful about our choices than he was.

Most of us will not be remembered beyond the lifetimes of those who knew us when they were young except as family photos may be reviewed at future family reunions, but we all leave a legacy. Our legacies will live for generations to come. For that reason it is wise to think carefully about how we want to be remembered and how others will be affected by our life choices.

If by reading this book you have been encouraged to embrace a missing dimension in your life or to eliminate a counterproductive behavior, regardless of your age, do it without hesitation. If you are middle age or older, remember, it's OK to be a late starter. Keep in mind that the story of your life is unlike that of anyone who has ever lived before you because of the family in which you were born and the century and the country in which you live. You also have a unique genetic makeup. Applications of the wisdom you gain from *Ecclesiastes,* therefore, will not look exactly like those of others around you. That's important in terms of what to expect both of yourself and of others, including members of your family.

Though no person has total autonomy in life, you are in control of your responses to life situations, either chosen or imposed upon you. Sometimes you can change the circumstances you are in, sometimes you can't. So pick the areas of your life where you can initiate action to make life better. Small changes make big differences. And for life circumstances beyond your control, focus on managing and enduring them. That will yield the best results for a good life in your imperfect world.

May the peace and the wisdom of God accompany you throughout life. Most of all, may you seek to make *"everything beautiful in its time"* and capture for yourself and those close to you the remnants of the life in Eden that are still available. Here's to a good life in spite of a messy world!

"O Lord Almighty, blessed is the man who trusts in you."
Psalm 84:12.

APPENDIX

RECIPES

- Bold and Classy Color Contrast Strawberry and Spinach Salad
- Melt in Your Mouth Boxing Day Beef Brisket
- Anna's *Bigos*, the National Dish of Poland

Bold and Classy Color Contrast Strawberry and Spinach Salad

Ingredients

- 1 lb. Spinach, chilled
- 1 lb. Strawberries, chilled
- Dressing:
    - 1 cup Mayo
    - ¼ cup Apple Cider
    - ¼ cup Sweetener (sugar, honey, or Agave nectar)
    - Poppy Seeds

Directions

- Make dressing ahead, chill, and dress salad before serving
- Some hostesses add blueberries and mango for a multi-colored presentation

Melt in Your Mouth Boxing Day Beef Brisket
Day 1

Directions

- Place
    - 5 lbs. of beef brisket
    - ½ bottle Girard's Champagne dressing
    - ¾ cup rice seasoned vinegar

    in Pyrex dish marinate brisket overnight, turning a couple of times

Day 2

Directions

- Preheat oven to 300 degrees and discard dressing
- Wrap meat tightly in heavy aluminum foil
- Place in baking dish and bake for 3 ½ hours
- Open foil and bake for ½ hour more
- Remove foil from meat and leave meat and juices in Pyrex dish

Day 3

Directions

- Early in day drain accumulated juices and save for sauce
- Then slice meat very thinly against the grain
- Place back in dish
- Combine:
    - 1-1½ cup meat juices
    - 1 cup plain barbecue sauce

Brisket, Day 3 (continued)

- ½ jar of 4 ounce cranberry chutney (Trader Joe's)
- Brown sugar and rice vinegar to taste (sweet/sour)
- Heat until sugar is dissolved
- Pour about half of save over sliced meat
- Cover with foil
- Bake at 300 degrees for 1 hour before it is served
- Heat up other half of sauce and add 1 cup of fresh cranberries until soft, but not mushy
- Arrange meat on platter and drizzle cranberry sauce over all
- Or leave it in Pyrex dish and pour sauce on top (not quite as attractive, but more sauce)

One brisket serves 10 to 14 people

Anna's *Bigos*, the National Dish of Poland

Ingredients
- 3 lbs. seasoned cooked pork (chops, country style ribs, etc.)
- 1 onion, chopped
- 1 sixteen-ounce jar of sauerkraut, rinsed and drained (reserve some juice)
- 4 cups shredded cabbage
- ½ cup sliced fresh mushrooms
- 1 bay leaf

Directions
- Season and bake pork meat, or brown chops on top of stove
- Cut up meat after cooked
- Sauté onions and mushrooms and set aside
- Cook sauerkraut and cabbage on top of stove with bay leaf and enough water or sauerkraut juice so that it will not stick to the pot. Cook about 1 hour, covered. Stir occasionally and add liquid if needed
- Add sautéed onions and mushrooms
- Season with salt, sugar, paprika to taste
- Continue cooking, covered, and stir to meld flavors
- Best served the next day after flavors develop

Other recipes also season with dry basil, salt, black pepper, caraway seeds, dash of Worcestershire sauce or chopped garlic.

NOTES

---

1 These accounts of human trafficking were researched in the Public Policy Department of William Jessup University, Rocklin, California in a capstone senior project. The goals of the research were to inform Americans about exploitation within US borders and to advance public policies to restrain such evil.

2 Arthur C. Brooks, Professor of Business and Government Policy at Syracuse University in New York, author of *Who Really Cares* (Basic Books, 2006) spent years researching giving trends in America. Even he was surprised by what he found. He discovered that on the average, Americans who are religiously active citizens who hold values advanced by conservatives, such as church attendance, two-parent families, and the Protestant Work Ethic, are more generous than liberals. Not only did they give generously to religious organizations, but they also led the way in giving to arts organizations and for organizations focused on social causes. Conservatives also donated more blood.

71650407R00113

Made in the USA
San Bernardino, CA
18 March 2018